Praise for

What Would Jesus Undo

"What would Jesus undo? According to Michael Boggs, Jesus would undo a lot that's being done in his name. Michael has traveled as a worship leader and artist, and in numerous conversations with friends—both believers and unbelievers—he's noticed how often Christians actually get in the way of the gospel. In his very thoughtful way, Michael points out some of these walls we've built and talks about how we can tear them down. And that's good news, both to those who have been locked out and to those of us who are locked in."

—**Mike Glenn**, senior pastor at Brentwood Baptist

"Michael Boggs hits the nail on the head with *What Would Jesus Undo*. Without judgment or condescension, he opens the reader's eyes to the reality of things that we as Christians do, based more in church culture than on biblical principles. Michael challenges us as believers to think outside of the box and, in turn, step outside of what we might consider 'the norm' to make a lasting impact."

—**Anthony Evans**, musician and worship leader

"As Christians, we should constantly ask ourselves, what *would* Jesus do. But Michael Boggs has challenged our faith journey in a new way as he calls us to ask, what would Jesus *undo*? I am a big fan of good and thought provoking questions, and Michael sets the stage for us to explore ways perhaps Jesus would *undo* some things we have done 'in his name.' Jesus always met and embraced the hurting and wounded—the weary and worn. He had a 'thing' for the under dogs! I am so glad he has offered me mercy and grace in my life. Jesus is the kind of Savior that's not afraid to get his hands dirty. So . . . what *would* Jesus undo?"

—**Sandi Patty**, most awarded female vocalist in Christian music history

WHAT
WOULD
«« JESUS
UNDO

WHAT WOULD «« JESUS UNDO

MICHAEL BOGGS

LEAFWOOD
PUBLISHERS
an imprint of Abilene Christian University Press

WHAT WOULD JESUS UNDO

L E A F W O O D
P U B L I S H E R S
an imprint of Abilene Christian University Press

LIBRARY OF CONGRESS CATALOGING-IN-PUBLICATION DATA
Boggs, Michael, 1978-
  What would Jesus undo / Michael Boggs.
    pages cm
  ISBN 978-0-89112-624-9
  1. Christianity and culture. 2. Distraction (Psychology)--Religious aspects. I. Title.
  BR115.C8B525 2014
  248.4--dc23
                                                                          2014015749

Cover design by Marc Whitaker
Interior text design by Sandy Armstrong

For information contact:
Abilene Christian University Press
1626 Campus Court
Abilene, Texas 79601

1-877-816-4455
www.leafwoodpublishers.com

14 15 16 17 18 19 / 7 6 5 4 3 2 1

To my beautiful wife, Keely:

Thank you for allowing me the privilege of
partnering with you in ministry as well as in life.
You're better than I deserve. You're more than I could
have asked for. I'll take every moment you give me.

Forgive others.
Forgive yourself.
Trust Christ.

Acknowledgments

I would like to thank the many pastors and teachers I get to listen to every week at home or on the road. I'm sure I probably am quoting you more than I realize, but at least that lets you know I am paying attention. Thank you for the words of life you speak each week.

I would like to thank Melissa Greene for sharing the WWJU phrase with me. I am grateful for your leadership and dedication to spreading the Good News. (You also sing like an angel!)

I would like to thank my manager, Mike Atkins, and acquisitions editor, Gary Myers. I never dreamed I would actually get to write a book about the things God is undoing in me. I guess I should watch what I say around you guys next time.

Finally, I would like to thank the London Symphony Orchestra for recording the *Braveheart* soundtrack. I listened to it nearly every day while I was writing this book.

Contents

The Origin of
What Would Jesus Undo

I heard a sermon recently that blew me away.

Yes, I know it's hard to believe, but worship leaders and musicians do pay attention to sermons. Most of the time.

I was leading worship at a youth conference in Pigeon Forge, Tennessee, when a well-known speaker named Shane Claiborne stepped onto the platform. I had never heard him before, so I was excited. I knew he had lived an interesting life and had made several sacrifices to walk with Jesus in a manner that wasn't common or expected of a Christian leader like himself.

He hit the stage that night wearing really baggy pants and dark-rimmed glasses. I'm usually pretty good at getting an accurate read on someone by just spending a few minutes with them. My first impression of him was that he was gentle and compassionate. He began to speak, and immediately I was engaged by his charisma. At some point during his message, I found myself on the edge of my seat as he cited statistics on how unchurched people view Christians. He was quoting a book called *Unchristian*. He said that several hundred non-Christians had been asked a simple question:

> *What are the first few things that come to your mind as you think about the word* Christian?

Their answers were alarming. The top three responses were antigay, hypocritical, and judgmental. Nothing good or positive made it into the top ten responses, and *love* never made the list. I literally said out loud, "Are you kidding me? *Love* never made the list? The Scriptures say that the world will know us by our love."

Brennan Manning is heard at the beginning of the dc Talk song "What If I Stumble" saying, "The greatest single cause of atheism in the world today is Christians who acknowledge Jesus with their lips, then walk out the door and deny Him by their lifestyle. That is what an unbelieving world simply finds unbelievable."

As I listened to Shane in Pigeon Forge that night, I was sad. I was troubled. I hated to think that this is how many non-Christians perceive the church. It upset me to the core of my being to realize how many people might never see God's love in us. And I recalled my pastor's frequent remark that "it seems as though we are most known by what we're against rather than what we're for."

That night I had to admit that he is right. Realizing this broke my heart. I had to do something about it. But what could a red-headed musician from Berryhill, Oklahoma, do about a problem so huge, so widespread?

Strange as it may seem, I got my question answered because of grilled chicken and a baked potato. That's what I was having for lunch at J. Alexander's one day while I was meeting with a worship leader friend of mine whom I deeply respect. She was catching me up on the latest series at her church, which they were calling *What Would Jesus Undo*. As she spoke that short phrase, my eyes lit up. I stopped her and said, "That's a great title!"

Several times I had asked myself the simple, popular question What Would Jesus Do? I had at least ten WWJD bracelets in junior high and high school. In assorted colors. (I was trying to be fashionable and spiritually conscious at the same time.) I had heard that question asked in a jillion sermons, but I had never thought about what Jesus would *undo.*

Jesus was already undoing something inside me, but I didn't know what yet. I walked away from lunch that day thinking about the sermon I had heard from Shane. What would Jesus undo about the way we Christians treat people, or about the way we act both inside and outside the church? More importantly, what would he undo in me concerning the way I represent him to a world that desperately needs him?

As I pursued this line of thinking, I began to research what Jesus sought to undo or change in the hearts and minds of the people he walked with and preached to. I found that Jesus tried to break down a lot of walls, and he fought to destroy certain ways of thinking. Exactly what did he try to change, and how can I help put those things in bold print so people, including myself, can learn to represent Jesus and his teachings in the best possible way?

If we're going to ask the question, What Would Jesus Undo, I believe it's best to look into Scripture and see what he tried to undo during his ministry on earth. We need to search for any parallels between his message then and our culture now. Study and research reveals so many parallels that one book can't possibly hold them all. Jesus would undo a lot. In the following pages we will examine some of the words of Jesus and then ask ourselves: What Would Jesus Undo?

(One helpful hint: first ask that question to yourself. I have found that it's very easy to point to others and preach about what Jesus would undo in them. Do your best to point that finger back at yourself.)

More Like a Lion, Less Like a Lamb

"I'd rather spend one day as a lion, than a thousand as a lamb."

—RICK PITINO

You might be asking yourself why on earth a worship leader/singer-songwriter would decide to write a book on such a controversial topic as *What Would Jesus Undo*. Wouldn't it make more sense to reserve a topic like this for a pastor or teacher who has years of experience and education? Who am I to write this book?

Believe me, all these questions have been rattling around in my brain for the past year as I have tried to put flesh on the bones of this idea. As a songwriter, I usually spend a lot of time developing ways to say something that allows for listener interpretation. I generally try my best to be artistic in the way I express my thoughts and ideas. In this case, however, I think I'd rather just be blunt. The answer to the WWJU question is actually pretty simple.

I believe God loves us with an intense, furious, and irreversible love that is not only meant to captivate our hearts but is also intended to flow through us to anyone and everyone with whom we come in contact. But it seems to me that while a lot of us claim to be followers of Jesus, too many of us never actually do the things he did or undo the things he tried to undo. We don't talk the way he talked or love the way he loved. Sometimes we are so eager to please ourselves (I include myself in this) that loving somebody who might be unlovable often seems too difficult and, honestly, just too much of an inconvenience.

We're far too busy to live as Jesus lived. He would interrupt his entire schedule just to eat lunch with outcasts like Zacchaeus. He would extend an invitation of friendship to people like Matthew, who was considered by most to be thief and a traitor. He would offer no condemnation to people who were actually caught in the act of sin—people like the woman who was almost stoned for committing adultery. He gave her help instead of hatred, blessing rather than blame.

When I look at the church in North America as a whole, I don't always see this kind of Jesus in us, and I don't always see him in me.

The first step toward fixing any problem is admitting you have one. So here I am admitting to you that I have a problem. I have lived a mostly Christian life. By "mostly Christian," I mean that I've kept most of the rules. I have a great attendance record at church, and I pay my tithes every month. I've been a worship leader, teacher, communion server, and prayer counselor. I've often studied into the wee hours of the morning in preparation for a devotional, a sermon, or a song. But even on my best days, some things about my life simply don't look like Jesus.

I know there is grace for mistakes—so much grace, in fact, that we could never out-sin the great depth of mercy God has for us. My faults are as numerous as the sand on Daytona Beach, but still God has more grace than I have sin. One of my favorite books, Henry van Dyke's *Valley of Vision,* echoes these sentiments: "O, if He would punish me for my sins, it would not wound my heart so deep to offend Him. But though I sin continually, He continually repeats His kindness to me" (126).

God constantly shows me grace, but this doesn't give me a license to sin. It's not an excuse to do whatever I want. It's not a reason to live a "mostly Christian" life. Is that what I want to tell God when I get to heaven? That I was "mostly Christian"?

I was caught off guard last year at a three-day prayer retreat with our staff at Brentwood Baptist Church in Nashville, Tennessee. We have one of these every year, but this was the first one I had been able to attend. I was told we would be doing a lot of praying and Scripture reading. Go figure. My friends who don't go to church think that's all I do anyway, because I work for God. One friend even joked, "Does God ever make you work overtime?" I responded by saying, "Yes, but the retirement benefits are out of this world." He didn't laugh. Not even a little smile.

Anyway, we arrived at the prayer retreat and quickly discovered this was going to be a different kind of experience for most of us. It involved our telling other staff members face-to-face what godly characteristics we saw in them. Tears flowed in some of those moments. We read and prayed Scripture over our co-workers and friends.

We also listened more than we actually talked during our prayer time. I can assure you that, for me, listening during prayer doesn't happen all that often, even though I want it to. I've got a long list of things that need to be said during prayer, and usually I don't have time, or I don't make time, to hear what God might say back to me about it. During one of those listening times, however, I felt like God began to speak to me.

God has spoken to my heart enough for me to know when it's him. So I got very quiet and just listened. As clear as a bell in a village church steeple, God said these words: "Michael, I want you to be more like a lion and less like a lamb."

Now, to give you some background, the Lord has used the image of a lion in my life several times to help encourage, embolden, and empower me. Oftentimes, God has used the traits of a lion to help me see what he sees in me. Most days, I assure you, I don't see a lion when I look in the mirror. I see a young man hanging on for dear life, trying to make sense of a senseless world. Nonetheless, during that moment of prayer,

God repeated to me: "Michael, I want you to be more like a lion and less like a lamb."

My first thought was, "What do you mean, Lord?" Lions are brave and fearless. They are known for their tenacity and ferociousness. Lambs have a reputation for being meek, passive, dumb, and most of the time scared of their own shadow. I had a feeling that God was doing something in my life that was going to change how I had lived up to that point. I just didn't know how he was going to change me from a lamb to a lion. Those are quite opposite animals.

To be completely honest, I may not have seen myself as a lion, but I didn't see myself as a lamb either. I didn't like to think of myself as a lamb. In my opinion, lambs seem weak. I played football and baseball in school and received scholarships to play those sports in college. I liked lifting weights, action movies, going camping, fishing, and watching UFC. Those were all pretty manly things. Lionlike things even—or so I thought.

But God wasn't concerned with what I did for fun. He was concerned with what I did for him. He was about to saturate my heart with Scriptures I had read a thousand times before but had never really understood. He was about to show me times when Jesus behaved like a lion and was completely determined to do what God asked him to despite what people thought or said about him. He was about to reveal to me what it looked like to be a lion. Ironically, just like a lamb, I was scared to death.

For accountability purposes, I told a few close friends about the "more like a lion, less like a lamb" phrase God had spoken to me at the retreat. Anytime they saw me behaving like a lamb, they had full permission to call me out on it. And they did. The first time it happened I was in a meeting at church where I had not spoken up when asked my honest opinion. My friend knew it. The meeting adjourned and my buddy told me that I should have said something. He encouraged me to correct it ASAP. He brought one of the individuals back into the room and nicely asked me to share my truthful feedback.

Pretty soon, my wife jumped on board the "more like a lion" train, pointing out to me a few times when I had chosen an easier or less challenging route. By the end of the first three months, I had never felt more like a lamb. My eyes were opened to how passive I was about certain things. I began to see that my desire to avoid conflict had begun to overshadow my desire to do what was right.

Quickly, I learned that being a lion could be hard. It required me to oppose ungodly things and not just go with the flow. It became absolutely necessary for me to start defending people who needed defending and to respectfully disagree with people with whom I didn't agree. It even required me to apologize to those people if later I found that I was wrong. It required that I live, love, and act like Jesus in every way possible. Being a lion required that I *do* something.

Almost a year after I heard the Lord speak that phrase to me, I read about a world-class basketball coach named Rick

Pitino who had made his mark at the University of Kentucky. He won so many basketball games that many say he is the greatest basketball coach of all time. Pitino left a lengthy career with Kentucky to take a job coaching in the NBA. After a short stint in the pros, he decided to return to college basketball. He had coaching offers from several colleges, but he had verbally committed to coach at the University of Michigan.

Pitino's wife wasn't happy with that decision, however. She wanted him to coach near Kentucky so they could be close to family and friends again, but Pitino didn't want to coach near Lexington. He realized that when you leave a successful program like Kentucky and then try to coach another team in close proximity, it can breed hatred against you. He thought the tried-and-true Kentucky fans would heckle him so much that it likely would be miserable to coach anywhere close to the Wildcats. He feared that his family would be rejected, and he didn't want to put them through that kind of hassle. During several lively discussions of these hard choices, Pitino's wife reminded him of how he was always telling his players a motivational phrase that he now seemed to have forgotten: "I'd rather spend one day as a lion than a thousand as a lamb."

In a rather colorful way, during their conversation, she called Pitino a lamb. He then did what every good husband does. He listened to his wife. He forfeited the coaching job at Michigan and took the job as the head basketball coach for the University of Louisville. There he won a national championship and further established his legacy as one of the best coaches of all time in college basketball.

Coach Pitino and I had one thing in common. Both of us were being challenged to be a lion. His challenge came in the arena of basketball, and mine came in the area of religion. I began writing, recording, and singing songs that previously made me apprehensive. I began asking God to replace my fear with bravery. I asked him to exchange my passiveness with boldness that led to action. I wanted him to change my attitude of someone-else-will-do-this to Lord-help-*me*-do-this. Those are scary prayers, my friends. Let's just say I am still a work in progress.

However, I agree with Pitino. I would rather spend one day as a lion than a thousand as a lamb.

In a nutshell, that's why I wrote the chapters that make up this book. They represent a young man doing his best to live a life that honors God and promotes the saving power of Jesus Christ. Jesus is our only hope. I need him more than I need air. I am conscious of that reality, and writing this book has forged my dependence on him more deeply than I've ever known before.

If you need to, I give you permission to get mad as you read this book. You probably will. Go ahead and throw your book at the wall. You might want to. Threaten to rid me of any opportunity to spread the concepts found in these pages. But I beg you, don't read this book and do nothing. If you agree that Jesus would undo certain things, then join him in undoing them. If you decide I am a heretic for what I say in this book, then point people in the way they should go. But don't sit there and do nothing.

My hope, however, is that inside these next chapters you'll begin to ask and answer some hard questions.

Is the way I'm living the way Christ lived?

Is my life pointing people in the right or wrong direction?

Am I in the way of people who need to get to Jesus?

I leave you with these poignant words from the great theologian, country singer Toby Keith, in his song "Love Me If You Can." I believe this sums up my prayer as I write these words today: "Hate me if you want to, but love me if you can."

Now, join me as we try to find out what a lion like Jesus would undo.

CHAPTER ONE

Walls

"We build too many walls and not enough bridges."

—Isaac Newton

What would Jesus undo? That is a loaded question.

When I asked friends, family, strangers, Christians, non-Christians, senior adults, kids, and just about everybody in between, I found that everyone has an opinion on what Jesus would undo. No one has said, "I don't know, let me think about it," or, "I'd like to ask someone else and get back with you." Everyone has an answer.

Some of the answers I expected. Some of them I did not. Politics, war, suffering, and abuse all made the list. Denominational lines, judgmentalism, hypocrisy, greed, and hunger were among some of the top responses. One of my friends said Jesus would undo his mother-in-law's cooking.

Ouch! But make no mistake, our neighbors have an idea of what Jesus would undo, and they aren't shy about expressing it.

One of my favorite responses came from a young man I got to know at the gym. He was a successful business owner who was skeptical about the whole Christian thing. After months of deliberation, however, he had given his life to Christ and was trying hard to follow Jesus. In his words, he was "overcoming a lot of demons," but he refused to let them take hold of him anymore. He had worked diligently at reading his Bible, attending a local church, and serving the poor in our city. As a friend, I was proud of him. As a minister, I wished everyone in the church would be as committed as this man.

One day at lunch I asked him, "What do you think Jesus would undo?"

He took the wrapper off his straw, put it into his Coke, and took a sip, then spoke these words loudly enough for the whole restaurant to hear: "I think Jesus would undo all the walls we [Christians] build. You know, the walls that keep us in and keep others [non-Christians] out. He would undo the walls we build inside our churches to separate one Christian from another. Jesus would undo walls."

I loved his response. It was bold and direct. I'm a bottom-line kind of guy, and that was a bottom-line kind of statement. I was a little surprised, though, by the depth of emotion in his answer. Whenever I ask someone this question, I pay close attention to what they say but even closer attention to the emotions they display while answering. He spoke honestly but with a hint of anger. I recognized that anger because I've seen the same ire in myself.

A counselor friend told me that often what is underneath mad is sad. In my case, that statement was dead on. I think the same was true of my gym friend as well. He was sad about a lot of things. Most of those things could be defined as walls or barriers that had separated him from God. Sometimes those walls were built by other people. Sometimes he built them on his own. At other times, it seemed as though they were built by Satan himself. One thing was absolutely certain that day. My friend wanted those walls torn down. Wrecked. Destroyed. Undone. His tears proved it.

We spent some time asking Jesus to break down those walls. He is now breaking down those walls, and I believe he will continue tearing them down until the day my friend meets our Lord face-to-face.

For Jesus-followers, every wall with evil intent will be gone in heaven. There will be nothing there to separate us from God. Nothing. My friend got emotional when we talked about that reality. I believe reactions like his are proof that "we were made for another world," as C. S. Lewis said in *Mere Christianity* (136).

But until that day, what do I do about these walls my friend was telling me about? Once I started thinking about it, walls seemed to be everywhere in our world. We have walls in our nation, in our churches, in our homes, in our relationships, and even in our own hearts.

Walls can serve several purposes, some good and some bad. Some walls provide defense, shelter, and refuge. All of those things, I'm pretty fond of. But some walls protect horrible things like racism, hatred, self-righteousness, hypocrisy, and Satan's all-time favorite, plain ole sin.

Those wicked walls need to come down. I believe Jesus wants to undo any wall that separates God from the people he loves. I also believe he wants us to join him in the "undoing" process.

Walls in Our Churches

This means we're going to have to discuss some difficult things in this book. First, we're going to talk about the walls that exist in our own churches.

Let me make one thing clear early in this book: I love the church. I'm a member of one. I work at one. I travel to several churches every year and do my best to encourage, support, and love the local church. I do not condone church-bashing in any way, shape, or form, and I don't intend to do any of it in these pages.

It's too easy in our culture, and especially among those in my generation, to get pulled into the "I love Jesus, but I don't like his church" mantra. One pastor I know pointed to the metaphor in Scripture that depicts God as the groom and the church as his bride. He said that claiming to love Jesus but not his church is like saying, "God, I like you but I hate your wife." I don't know any guy who would like for that to be said about his wife. Surely God doesn't like to hear it said about his bride either.

I believe that God not only likes the church, he loves it. We should love it, too.

With that said, let me further explain that I don't think loving, supporting, and serving the church means ignoring the fact that we still have a lot of work to do to bring the church up to God's standards. Simply put, we can use some improvement. A lot of it. Recognizing this doesn't make me an expert or a know-it-all. I don't claim to have a PhD in Church Walls. I'm just a guy who has tried to pay attention to my friends, both Christian and otherwise, when they talk about church. Specifically, when they tell me what frustrates them about church and its leadership. Here's one example.

Christians who in the name of God use hate to promote a message of love really don't have a healthy grasp on the gospel's actually being Good News. It really is "Good News"! Why do some believers seem to think that spewing hate is a good way to evangelize? I have never bought a vacuum cleaner because the salesman at the door told me he hated me, the company boss hated me, and everyone who ever sold vacuums hated me, so I should buy a vacuum. That's just plain asinine. Likewise, telling people God hates them in order to put them in their place and then convert them to Christianity is just as stupid. (Did I mention earlier that I was going to be blunt?)

Sometimes I hear preachers do this from the pulpit. Or it may be some misguided soul carrying a cardboard sign that says things I'm too ashamed to print in this book. Hate messages get delivered on the church pew, in the grocery store, on the ball field, and in coffee shops across the land. It even happens on boats.

Working as an eighteen-year-old Kanakuk Kamp Kounselor in Branson, Missouri (if you know anything about Kanakuk, you'll understand the spelling), I decided on one of my days off to take a tour of Table Rock Lake via pontoon boat. About thirty passengers climbed aboard on that summer day, eager to see all the beauty Table Rock had to offer. The captain was a jovial and upbeat fellow. Even though this was probably the one-millionth tour he had done on that lake, he didn't show it. When he was talking about this massive body of water, it was as if he was seeing it for the first time, just as many of us were.

Somewhere along the way we saw a huge rock structure that only could have been created by God. I think someone even said that. Then one of the passengers brought up religion. Specifically Christianity. She began to tell everyone that the Lord was coming back soon and if we didn't know him, we would all go to hell. She was brash, and it was a bit sudden, but I didn't disagree with her. Maybe she was doing what she thought was right. But she kept going and going and going. The captain was silent, but I could tell that he didn't want this woman and her religious viewpoints to ruin the tour for everyone.

The lady continued but the content of her impromptu sermon kept getting worse. She began naming all the celebrities she thought were going to hell. Madonna, Donald Trump, and some magician she didn't like all made the cut. People grew tired of her tirade, and any credibility Christianity had with unbelievers on that boat got soiled by this overly zealous lady.

Eventually, the captain told her he appreciated her views but also appreciated the fact that we live in a country where we have the freedom to choose what we believe and practice concerning religion. He was gracious in his response to her, but she furiously turned to him and barked, "Don't tell me you're not a Christian!"

I can't remember exactly what he replied, but his response was respectful. In essence, he said he was still searching. Let's just say it escalated from there. She started in with her sermon again, only this time she increased the volume about one hundred decibels. She started describing to this man the agony of hell, and then she asked him if he wanted to burn forever. Her face grew red and angry. Instead of being flustered, the captain began to smile because this out-of-control woman was getting so worked up. His amusement set her off even more. She started yelling. I couldn't get off that boat fast enough. I was embarrassed to be there.

Finally, the lady cooled down a bit and for about ten minutes her fire-filled homily was reduced to an irritating mutter. When the tour was over and everybody had left, I apologized to the boat captain. I was sorry for so many things. I was sorry for the things the lady had said. I was sorry that all the folks on the boat had to endure her ranting and raving. I was sorry that a conversation about a good God and the beauty he creates turned into a speech that included lines like, "I hope you like hot weather, brother." It still makes my stomach sick to even think about it. The captain smiled and said, "That's okay. She's not the first, and she probably won't be the last." Ugh.

Don't misunderstand my point in sharing this awful story. I believe in hell. I understand the power of evil spiritual forces and the destruction they cause in people's lives. I realize a tension exists in loving someone while we recognize, assess, and deal with his sins. I'm aware of and fully support the truth that repentance and salvation through Jesus Christ are the only way to have a right relationship with God. Only by his mercy and grace are we allowed the possibility of walking into heaven one day and calling it home. I believe these things with all my heart. I just don't think the best way to convince someone he needs Jesus is through preaching hate. God doesn't hate us. He loves us. John 3:16 explains this concept plainly. "God so loved the world that he gave his one and only Son, that whoever believes in him shall not perish but have eternal life."

God's love for us doesn't depend on who we are, but that we are. If you are alive, God loves you and wants a relationship with you. I wish more of my friends who are not Christ-followers would hear that message from Christians. Instead, some of them are constantly bombarded with angry sermons by hateful believers who simply want to bully them to Jesus. I don't want us to preach a weak gospel; but in my Bible, I never read about Jesus forcing someone to follow him. It's always a choice. It's a good choice but, nevertheless, a choice.

Honestly, church people create many walls. The one I just described is only one of them. I don't claim that I have identified them all, but I've had too many discussions with folks who are hurt, tired, empty, and jaded. It tells me that real barriers exist and need to come down if we wish to reach people with the Good News of Jesus Christ. We'll discover some more of these walls Christians have erected in the church and discuss the ways we can help break them down.

Walls in Our Lives

Other walls block the message of Jesus outside of the church. Many of those walls are inside of us. These walls are a direct result of our enemy and his strategies to distract and neutralize us here on earth. An example of one of those many walls is worry.

Have you noticed that worry just gives birth to more worry? It's like a snowball rolling downhill. As long as it keeps rolling, it grows bigger and bigger. Eventually it gets out of control and begins to destroy everything in its path. Sound familiar?

Worry also tells us to focus only on worst-case scenarios. When my wife, Keely, and I go down the road of worrying out loud, which happens way too often, usually one of us will jokingly refer to *Jeopardy* and say, "I'll take Worst-case Scenarios for $500, Alex." That bit of humor is kind of like a reset button. We laugh about it because we've both been caught up in this. We find each other making up alternate universes that contain the worst possible outcomes. Keely and I know all the "don't worry" verses. We've memorized most of them. We practically have a doctorate in the study of not worrying, yet at times we find ourselves adding brick after brick to the wall of worry.

Worry's objective is to make sure that wall rises so high that we won't be able to see God. We won't be able to hear him. If we're not careful, we might forget he's even there. Jesus is working on the other side of that wall, however, undoing every brick we put up. He's aggressively taking a hammer to any wall that separates us from God. In Matthew 6:25–34 he gives us these words to help break down those walls of worry:

> Therefore I tell you, do not worry about your life, what you will eat or drink; or about your body, what you will wear. Is not life more than food, and the body more than clothes? Look at the birds of the air; they do not sow or reap or store away in barns, and yet your heavenly Father feeds them. Are you not much more valuable than they? Can any one of you by worrying add a single hour to your life?
>
> And why do you worry about clothes? See how the flowers of the field grow. They do not labor or spin. Yet I tell you that not even Solomon in all his splendor was dressed like one of these. If that is how God clothes the grass of the field, which is here today and tomorrow is thrown into the fire, will he not much more clothe you—you of little faith? So do not worry, saying, "What shall we eat?" or "What shall we drink?" or "What shall we wear?" For the pagans run after all these things, and your heavenly Father knows that you need them. But seek first his kingdom and his righteousness, and all these things

will be given to you as well. Therefore do not worry
about tomorrow, for tomorrow will worry about
itself. Each day has enough trouble of its own.

According to Jesus, if you have a worry problem, you have a
God-focus problem. Defeating worry is as simple as shifting
your attention to the One who can do something about the
things you're worried about. Instead, we sometimes let worry
run away with our thoughts. We make it Priority Number One
instead of making God and his kingdom what matters most in
our lives.

God is patient and loving. He knows we face these walls.
We read in the New Testament about Jesus facing some of
these walls. God will help us break through them, but we
have to want them to come down. We have to want to live in a
world without such barriers. Too often, I fear, we learn to live
with them. We say things like, "They've always been there;
it probably will never change." Or, "That's just part of what
I struggle with." Nonsense. "We are more than conquerors"
through Jesus Christ our Savior (Rom. 8:37). You and I can
bless ourselves as well as the next generation by undoing some
of these walls in our churches and in our lives.

Tearing Down the Walls

As I was contemplating our life-constricting, faith-limiting
walls, I began to ponder some of the famous walls around the
world. One of the most interesting to me was the Berlin Wall.
In 1961, the Communist government began to construct a

wall that would separate East and West Berlin. Roads were blocked. Underground railways were barricaded and eventually rerouted so that few people could pass from one sector to the other. The German Democratic Republic made it impossible to get from one side to the other without jumping through a million hoops.

Some people thought a wall like that would never come down. But on November 9, 1989, the East German Communist Party announced that the wall that had separated the two Germanies for almost forty years would be destroyed. Excitement swept both halves of the city. Celebrations erupted. Soon people flooded the streets with hammers and pickaxes and began chipping away at the wall that for so long had kept them from seeing what life was like on the other side.

I can't help but think that we should take a hammer to the unnecessary walls in our churches and in our lives too. It's time for us to start breaking through some of those barriers that we thought would never come down. We just might find that life on the other side of that wall is better than anything we could imagine.

My friend was right at lunch that day. Jesus would undo walls. Now, let the undoing begin.

CHAPTER TWO

Greed

*"If Christ were here now,
there is one thing he would not be—a Christian."*

—Mark Twain

I'm not sure I agree with Twain, but I do understand his point. Christianity has a bad reputation in many circles. Some think we Christians are too legalistic; others think we are too lenient. We're too judgmental to suit some folks, too gracious to please others. We're too Republican or too Democrat, depending on the observer.

We hear all of these things cited as reasons why people don't want anything to do with church. Sometimes they're just excuses. Many times, unfortunately, they are not. Some will even tell you that their repugnance to Christianity has nothing to do with their not wanting to be religious or spiritual. Many of them don't have a problem with Jesus. In fact most people like Jesus. They simply don't see Christ in the Christians they know. Remember what Ghandi reportedly said? "I like your Christ, but I don't like your Christians. Your Christians are so unlike your Christ."

Have I made you nervous by quoting Mark Twain and Mahatma Ghandi in the opening lines of this chapter? I did it to make a point.

Many of our friends, family, and co-workers are not buying into Christianity because of us. Because of us Christians.

One meaning of the word *Christian* is "little Christ." If we Christians were to look at our lives, would we see a "little Christ"? Or would we see "very little Christ"? Unfortunately for me, even though I'm embarrassed to admit it, I sometimes feel that the answer would be the latter.

It was no different in the time of Jesus. While he was preaching and teaching in the name of God to bring others to God, the Pharisees were claiming to do the same thing. But Jesus had a very different view than they did on what a follower of God actually should be and do. Jesus had a few explosive moments of conflict with some of the religious leaders. In his book *Accidental Pharisees,* Larry Osborne refers to those guys as "Jesus Jerks." Whatever you want to call them, Jesus confronted them in order to undo some things inside the church system. The changes he advocated would cause a major disruption to the religious society of his day.

Deception and Disappointment

Speaking of disruption to society, let me tell you a little about my childhood. I didn't get into a lot of trouble as a kid, but I was a bit mischievous. My parents were pretty strict so I didn't break the rules too often, but every now and then it seemed like a good idea.

When I was about fourteen years old, I thought I might be able to sneak something past my parents. I had been invited to a party by some of my older friends. I asked my parents nicely if I could go. I told them all the reasons it would be a good idea for me to attend this party. I even told them all my Christian friends would be there. That was always a good reason in my parents' eyes. I had even come up with a way to work for my parents the next day just in case that would help sway their decision to let me go.

Without much deliberation, however, they said no. They really didn't need to give me a reason why. I knew why. They didn't want me hanging out with certain kids because they thought they were a bad influence on me. Needless to say, I was pretty upset. I had friends, important friends, who were going to be at this party, and I was convinced that if I didn't show up, it would probably ruin my entire junior high and high school experience. At least, that's what I told myself.

So, I hatched a plan with a friend. We were going to sneak out. Now this had to be carefully concocted because my parents were like FBI agents. They somehow knew every move I was going to make before I made it. They knew what I was thinking before I thought it. They were experts on one subject: me.

All that day I was nervous. I had gone over the plan a million times in my head. What would happen if I got caught? What would happen if my mom woke up to come check on me during the night and I wasn't there? But those valid questions were not enough to keep me from doing something stupid. If I could just stop time and somehow go back to that moment, I would tell myself this was a bad idea. But, alas, I can't. So the story continues.

Around midnight I got a page. Yes, that's when pagers were hip and trendy, like skinny jeans and Wayfarers are now. The page was from my buddy Will telling me he was on his way. I asked my sister to turn on her hairdryer. I know that sounds strange, but it was common for my sister to go to sleep to the sound of a hairdryer. Don't ask why; I don't have room here to explain that one.

The plan was in motion. Slowly I raised my window. When I did, I could hear the sound of a four-wheeler in the distance. Then it shut off. He was close. Since my parents had a one-story ranch house, the next part was easy. I simply climbed out of my bedroom window and walked briskly through the wet grass to the edge of the concrete driveway. It seemed like an eternity, but eventually Will pushed the four-wheeler through the dark to my parents' driveway. He had shut off the loud engine so it wouldn't wake up my parents. We high-fived each other. Then I took one side and he took the other, and we pushed our getaway vehicle down the road about a hundred yards.

Then Will said, "This is far enough." We both got on and, with one crank of the motor, we were on our way.

He was driving. I was riding on the back. He only had one helmet, which he generously gave to me since I was younger than he was by a couple of years. It made sense to me, so I put it on.

We had a few hurdles left to jump though. We had left from my parents' house undetected, but we had to traverse a fairly long stretch of road that was well traveled at night. A four-wheeler on that road in our little town was sure to be spotted. Probably by someone we knew. Or even worse, by someone who knew our parents.

We had to be invisible. We had to be stealthy with military precision. We tried driving on the side of the road, which we were pretty sure was mostly grass. We turned off the head-lights so we wouldn't attract attention to ourselves. The only problem with that was that we couldn't see where we were going. In fact, we couldn't even see our hands in front of our faces most of the time.

As we were cautiously but impatiently rolling down the dark road, suddenly Will hit the brakes as hard as he could. From my vantage point on the back of the ATV, I couldn't see it at the time, but we were headed straight for a huge hole. He tried the best he could to avoid it, but we plunged straight into that giant crevice in the ground. Both of us fell off. We shook our heads a little. We stood up. Eventually we realized that, although we had a few scratches on us, neither of us had been hurt badly and the four-wheeler was still operational. So we hopped back on and decided this time simply to drive on the road with our lights off.

My buddy and I headed toward one of the few intersections in Berryhill, Oklahoma. Until then, even with our wreck, we somehow had still managed to be completely unnoticed.

As we slowly made our ascent up a hill, we spotted the entrance to the subdivision. But that's not all we saw. Trouble was just ahead. A police car had just pulled out onto the road we were traveling on. Both of us knew things wouldn't be good if that cop got a glimpse of us. We did the only thing we could. We shut the four-wheeler off for a few moments and sat on the side of the road. The police car passed us, but something didn't feel right.

That's when it happened.

Will started the four-wheeler before the cop was completely out of sight. When he did, the headlights on the four-wheeler automatically came on. That wasn't supposed to happen. I turned around quickly and I could still see the police car in the distance. He had stopped and then made a U-turn in the middle of the street. Uh oh! He had spotted us. He turned on his flashing lights and siren and dashed toward us.

I have no idea what got into Will, but he started driving that four-wheeler like we had just robbed a bank. He was accelerating and shifting gears. If we were being filmed, this scene would wind up on a highlight reel. Two teenagers trying to evade a police car while driving an off-road vehicle at high speed. Talk about stupid . . .

Not far ahead lay a large wooded area where the cop car couldn't go. Will headed straight for it. We were going what seemed like 110 miles per hour. We were weaving in and out of bushes and trees. Honestly, I didn't even look back to see where the cop was because I was too busy hanging on for dear life.

I remember thinking, "Where did he learn to drive like this? Are we going to be on an episode of *Cops*? Why didn't he just stop when the cop turned his lights on?" That's probably when I would have waved the white flag, but not Will. I liked him for that. He took risks and I didn't. He was going to this party and, if I could hang on, I was too.

I couldn't believe it but as I looked back over my shoulder, I couldn't see the cop or his flashing blue and white lights anymore.

I yelled at Will, "I think we lost 'em, man."

Did I really just say that? Did we really just lose a cop? Who was I and what happened to that good little red-headed boy whose parents would kill him if they ever found out about this escapade?

It didn't matter now, though. We had successfully made it from my house, down a well-traveled road, past a cop, through the forest, and to the party. We could hear music playing as we got closer to our friend's house. Eventually, we found everybody standing outside by the street.

We *had* to tell our friends the story of what had just happened. When we did, our friends seemed mesmerized. Our reputation went up a few notches. We had racked up some cool points. The night was still young, and so were we. What did the rest of the night have in store?

Honestly? I can't remember much of what we did that night. I know we mostly talked with our friends. We stayed a few hours, but both Will and I knew we had to make that same trip all the way back to my house. So eventually we decided it was time to head home. I won't bore you with all the details of getting back across town, but we made it. No cops. No tipping the four-wheeler over. Just sheer execution. It was impressive.

I climbed back inside through the window of my bedroom. I changed into some gym shorts and a T-shirt and hopped in bed. Will paged me to let me know he got home safely and that his parents were sound asleep as well. Now I could finally get some sleep. Our mission had been successful. It didn't feel good though. Something was wrong about what I had done.

When I woke up the next day, my mom greeted me with the usual southern motherly question: "What do you want for breakfast, Sweetie?"

I'm not entirely sure what I requested, but I probably said cinnamon toast, since that was my favorite. My sister looked over at me and rolled her eyes.

She was the really good child. She was a straight-A student who would be the valedictorian of her class. Which by the way, I actually had to look up how to spell while typing this. She was a great athlete and also wore the crown as homecoming queen during her senior year. I was, to put it nicely, more playful than my sister. I had gotten away with a big no-no in our family. Sneaking out was punishable by death, as I would soon find out. I gloated in front of her. I even showed her a big scratch from the four-wheeler accident the night before. "It worked like a charm, Sis," I wanted her to know.

But in just a few hours it all came crashing down on me.

Sometime during the afternoon the phone rang. It was for me. I picked up the phone and said hello. I wasn't prepared for what would happen next.

The call was from the dad of the girl who threw the party the night before. He had heard that Will and I sneaked out of the house to come to the party. He also knew our parents would not approve of such behavior. He then said the words no teenager wants to hear: "Either you can tell your parents, or I will, but they need to know today."

This was the worst possible news I could get. I had gotten away with this whole shenanigan and now, in the midst of victory, I was going to have to confess what I had done? My heart sank.

I knew my parents well enough to know that I needed to be the one to tell them. So I mustered up my courage, took a deep breath, and told my parents we needed to talk.

All three of us walked out into the garage connected to our house. This is where we had important conversations. Mostly that was because my dad smoked cigarettes and Mom wouldn't let him smoke in the house. She said it turned the walls yellow, and she was right. I suspected that Dad was going to need a few hundred cigarettes over the next several minutes while I confessed my sins.

Then I spilled my guts.

I told them how I had deceived them, how I had slipped out of the house and gone to the party after they told me not to. I also told them about the girl's dad who had called and told me I needed to be honest with them about what I had done.

My mom started crying. Perfect. I kind of expected that from her, but I didn't expect it to hurt me so much. It was terribly upsetting to watch her realize that her son would, in fact, do something like this. The worst was yet to come, though.

My dad bypassed sad and went straight to mad. He said all the things I thought he would. But I wasn't prepared for that look in his eye. It was a look of shock but, even worse, disappointment. The look that says, "You let me down." The one that says, "I don't trust you any farther than I can throw you." And I was pretty sure he wanted to throw me somewhere. I hated that look. It was awful.

My parents asked me to leave while they talked about my punishment. This was not a good sign. They had never done that before. After about thirty minutes, they asked me to come back into the garage because they had decided on my fate. They were going to be generous and let me live. They also were going to ground me for a year.

Yep, that's right. A whole year! Three hundred sixty-five days. No talking on the phone. No hanging out with friends after school. No staying the night with buddies. Nothing. My calendar consisted of going to school and then coming home. Every day for a year. My life was over.

What makes the story even worse is that during my sentencing in the garage, the father of the girl called back. When

I answered the phone, he told me he was kidding about telling my parents and that he just wanted to scare me so I wouldn't do it again. It was too late, though. My judgment had already been pronounced. I was guilty as charged.

It was tragic. My friends laughed at me when I told them about my punishment. They reminded me how stupid I was for doing such a thing. My sister, being the good-hearted person she was, even tried to help me get out of some of the punishment, but not even her good reputation was going to help me with this one.

My parents stuck to their word for the most part. I stayed grounded for fifty weeks. They let me off two weeks early for good behavior. That even makes me laugh. What was I going to do, turn the TV up too loud? Think bad thoughts?

Looking back on it now, it's easy to see what the worst part of this whole story was. It wasn't being grounded for a year. It wasn't the lack of social life. It wasn't even the ridicule I received from my friends.

The worst punishment of all was that look on my dad's face. The look of disappointment. The look of "I can't believe you did that." I had displeased my father. The thought of that still bothers me today.

Undoing Greed in Holy Places

If Matthew 21:12–14 could provide us a glimpse at our Lord's facial expression, I believe it would have the same one my dad had all those years ago. Disappointment. Distrust. Unbelief. Anger.

Today, when we see a painting of Jesus, he usually has a glow about him. Most of the time he is smiling. He has a white, slightly tanned face. His hair is highlighted blond, and it's long and flowing. Some artists paint him so that his pose looks like it was from a senior-picture photo shoot. Sometimes he's carrying a lamb over his shoulder. Sometimes a child is sitting on his lap. Generally speaking, Jesus looks very peaceful. However, that's not the picture of Jesus found in the Scripture below. He is angry.

> Jesus went straight to the Temple and threw out everyone who had set up shop, buying and selling. He kicked over the tables of loan sharks and the stalls of dove merchants. He quoted this text:
>
> > My house was designated a house of prayer;
> > You have made it a hangout for thieves.
>
> Now there was room for the blind and crippled to get in. They came to Jesus and he healed them. (Matt. 21:12–14 MSG)

Just for a second, try to imagine this moment. Jesus, the Son of God, furiously walked into the temple, which was the epicenter of power in that culture. The temple was where political, economic, financial, and spiritual worlds coalesced. Then Jesus did the unthinkable. He started turning over tables and chasing people out of the temple. Christ was angered by what he saw in the temple that day.

Why was he so upset? The temple was a place of power, wealth, and religion. Today it might be like combining the White House, Wall Street, and the Vatican, then putting them under the same roof with one final authority that was subject only to the Roman government. The temple was God's house. It would be protected at all costs, even if that meant protecting it from the Son of God himself.

The temple was also the place where Jews from many parts of the world would come to offer their sacrifices to God to atone for their sins, to pay the yearly temple tax, to celebrate the annual feasts, and to worship God.

Unfortunately, some of the people in charge wanted to take advantage of these worshipers. The religious leaders had the market cornered with the temple. People wanted to worship God, and they also wanted to have their sins removed. They would pay whatever it might cost to do so, and the religious leaders knew that. They saw an opportunity to capitalize on these "sinners" while they were there. These corrupt leaders were greedy.

Inside the temple was a place called the Court of the Gentiles. This is where the money changers had set up business. This is where Jesus turned over the tables and started undoing a few things.

The reason for the money changers was completely ethical and logical. The temple only accepted a certain kind of coin, called a shekel. So when people from different parts of the world traveled to Jerusalem to go to the temple, they needed to exchange their money for shekels. This was completely legitimate, a necessary operation of the temple. What wasn't necessary was the high exchange rates these money changers were charging. According to historian Alfred Edersheim, in some cases the fees were "astronomic." Undoubtedly some people couldn't afford to offer their best sacrifices to God. To put it another way, they were simply too poor to worship God the way they wanted to.

We began this chapter by pointing out that Jesus will undo any wall that stands between his Father and the people he loves. One of those walls in Matthew 21 is greed. Greed of any kind is unacceptable, but especially greed in the name of God.

As defined by a friend of mine, greed is a desire for things beyond God's provision. Greed says, "What I have is not enough. I need more." Most of us know, of course, that having more is never enough. It may temporarily bring pleasure, but greed usually comes back with a bigger appetite.

Greed causes us to say and do stupid things. Good people have stolen because of greed. Good people have lied because of greed. That's what the religious leaders were doing in the temple. Jesus accused them of turning God's holy temple into a den of thieves. Wow!

We can be greedy for many reasons, but the bottom line on greed is that we think "'we need more to be more." What we own makes a statement about who we are. If we can accumulate more and more stuff, we can be who we think we ought to be. This kind of thinking is a trick of the enemy. As I said earlier, more is never enough. Wise Christian teachers have often pointed out that we should own our stuff and not let our stuff own us. Those religious leaders in Jesus' day began loving their wealth more than they loved the One who owns "the cattle on a thousand hills" (Ps. 50:10).

The antidote for greed is generosity. If you feel like you struggle with greed, start giving stuff away. Give away your time, your talents, and your treasures. Sure, it's going to be hard. But something about generosity begins to break down the wall of greed. How can you be greedy if you live a life with open hands? Oh, to live a life where we understand that everything we have is given by God and is his to use at any point he wants for his purposes and not our own.

I remember hearing a story about a monkey who put his hand into a trap to grab a couple of cubes of sugar. As long as his hand was closed, gripping a sugar cube, he couldn't remove it from the trap. The minute he opened his hand and released the sugar cube, he could pull out his hand. That monkey refused to let go of that sugar cube. He simply could not turn it loose. Because of his greed, the monkey stayed trapped until the hunters came back for him the next day.

I know it's a simple story, but sometimes I feel like that monkey with my hand in the trap. I'm unable to let go of certain things I need to release. I doubt that I am unique in this. Greed shows up in us all. It shows up in our relationships when we long for a friend's new car or their bigger house. It shows up in our relationships when we see how God is blessing someone else but doesn't seem to bless us in the same manner. It shows up in our thoughts when we begin to dream of a bigger bank account so we can indulge ourselves with it.

Greed is everywhere. If you're not careful, it will wrap its tentacles around our throats and begin to choke the life out of us. That's what greed does. It strangles every bit of joy and happiness in our thoughts. It cuts off the circulation of love flowing from God, through you, to others. Greed kills. That's why Jesus wanted it banished from the temple that day. It was killing the prayer and purity of God's house. It was killing people's ability to connect with God.

Jesus was adamant about tearing down walls that made it harder for people to get to God. Making it difficult on potential worshipers was the exact opposite of what those temple leaders should have been doing. They were supposed to help people get to God. Their job was to connect worshipers with a holy and good God who had been faithful to lead them out of Egypt, to deliver them from slavery, and to establish them as a chosen people loved by God. Instead, those religious leaders set an agenda to feed their own insatiable desire to make money and still look good while doing it. Like I said, greed will make people do stupid things.

What Jesus Cares About

Another important principle surfaces here. Notice that Jesus is not just upset with the people who put these walls of greed in place. He's also upset with the people who did nothing to tear them down.

The money changers were more than likely instructed and trained on how to take advantage of the people financially. In fact, most scholars agree that the money changers were getting some kind of kickback from all the earnings the temple was receiving. What would have happened if just one of the money changers had spoken up? What if one of them had said, "Guys, this isn't right. God wouldn't like this happening in his house. We need to stop"?

I don't know what would have happened, because we have no record of anything like that being said. No one stood up on behalf of the people. No one defended those who were being cheated. No one came to the rescue. No one but Jesus.

This wasn't the best way for a candidate to campaign for Savior of the World. This was not the best way to prove, "I'm God's Son." This certainly wasn't a way for Jesus to gain favor with the church or its leaders. No marketing executive in their right mind would have recommended this as a strategy to achieve popularity with the powers in the temple. But this didn't seem to bother Jesus. He simply didn't care about his own success or popularity. But he did care a lot about something else.

Jesus cared more about what his Father thought than about anyone else's opinion.

He cared more about the people who were being taken advantage of in his Father's house.

Jesus cared more for the sinners than he did for the self-proclaimed saints.

That day Jesus was trying to tell the temple leaders that what they were doing was wrong and against God's commands.

I don't know if the temple had meetings like my church does, but I do know that in my world Jesus' challenge to the money changing and the animal sales would have caused a plethora of meetings. In the hours that followed, there would have been meetings out the wazoo. We would have met for weeks about this radical preacher named Jesus who needed anger management classes.

Jesus was angry. He wasn't shy or scared. He was determined to undo something that was keeping people from God.

Are you okay with the idea that Jesus got mad? In our society anger is something that needs to be disciplined or controlled, even if it's for the right reasons. If we get riled, we are told to calm down and get ahold of ourselves. No minister in this generation can afford to lose his temper.

Being mad is not a luxury most Christians can afford. Or can we? Can we be angry at injustice? Can we be upset about people who are taken advantage of? You bet we can. No, we shouldn't sin in our anger. That is what Ephesians 4:26 tells us. The Bible is clear about that. But Jesus models a healthy way for us to be angry.

Has this ever happened to you? Have you ever spoken up about something that went against years of tradition? Traditions aren't necessarily bad things. They can help foster community, common language, and a sense of security. When those traditions become barriers between God and his people, however, they need to go. Have you ever opposed a tradition that you knew was a barrier to healthy faith? If so, you're in good company. Jesus did too.

Maybe you've observed certain traditions or people who stand in the way of others finding God. Maybe you have watched religious leaders who simply do nothing about the barriers that keep people from God. Maybe you've been one of those people yourself.

This may be a good place to stop and pray. If you want to, would you voice something like this prayer with me?

Lord Jesus, turn over the table of greed in my life.
Break down any wall that keeps others from you. Just
like you did in the temple, Lord, rush into my heart
and make it a holy place that is pleasing in your eyes.
Also grant me the wisdom and courage to remove any
barriers that keep others from you. Amen.

Neglect

"We think sometimes that poverty is only being hungry, naked, and homeless. The poverty of being unwanted, unloved, and uncared for is the greatest poverty."

—Mother Teresa

I believe Jesus wants to undo any barrier that stands between his Father and the people he loves. He started by turning over the tables of greed in the temple, but he didn't stop there. What I imagine to be a look of anger on the face of Jesus quickly turned into something much softer in the latter half of this story. In the same scene when we see our Lord's righteous indignation and his violent disapproval, Jesus also showed compassion to people who were hurting.

Jesus was always in control of his emotions. This doesn't mean he was not emotional. This doesn't mean he didn't have strong feelings. He just never allowed them to rule his actions. I've heard it said that emotions make wonderful passengers but horrible drivers. Even though Jesus was fully human, he bridled his feelings and made them submit to the lordship of his Father's will.

One of the many things I appreciate about Jesus is the way he treated others in the midst of an emotional roller coaster. Without doubt, his actions in the courtyard that day were highly charged with emotion. But this didn't keep him from seeing people who needed help. People who were hurting. People who were suffering. People who wanted someone, anyone, to love them enough to help them. So Jesus, who would soon be well acquainted with suffering, reached out to them in their distress. Thus he broke down another wall—the wall of neglecting the needs of others.

The Scriptures tell us that Jesus noticed a group of people inside the temple. These people weren't rich or upper class. They weren't popular or looked up to. They weren't even on most people's radars. These fringe people were blind and crippled.

More Precious Than Gold

I remember being on tour several years ago with FFH (a contemporary Christian band sometimes known as Far From Home). We were touring to promote our third record and were starting to enjoy the benefits of hard work and dedication to our ministry and music. Christian radio was playing our music, and people were actually showing up at our concerts to hear us play. Those were exciting days. It was a lot of fun for a twenty-three-year-old country boy from Oklahoma. I was just glad to be able to lead worship and perform music as my job. I couldn't believe I actually got paid to do what I loved.

We were playing a show somewhere in the northeast during the winter. The bus pulled up to the venue early that morning. I decided to go for a jog along the banks of a nearby river. I had just bought a new Nike running suit and running shoes, and I wanted to try them out. About ten minutes into my jog, I was crossing a small wooden bridge when I noticed a man sitting on the ground near the edge of the water. I wondered if he was homeless. Once I got close enough to see him better, it was evident that he was.

I kept running, but I couldn't keep from wondering if the man was okay. He didn't look okay. Eventually, I passed right above him on the bridge. I didn't get too far down the path before I heard that still small voice inside of me encouraging me go back and talk to the man.

I was a little apprehensive. Maybe I was afraid. Maybe I was selfish. Maybe I didn't want to bother the man. Whatever the case, I really didn't want to go down to where this guy was sprawled out on the ground. With a little more prompting from the Holy Spirit, however, I decided it was the right thing to do. I'm really glad I did.

I don't remember exactly how the conversation started, but at some point I asked him how he was doing. It was lame, but it at least started the dialogue. He wasn't doing well, but he smiled and said, "I've been better." That was easy to see. I felt like an idiot. He had obviously slept outside the night before, and probably several nights before that. His clothes were dirty and smelled like a trashcan. His beard was matted, and to this day I can still see part of a spider web girdling that beard. Of course, he had been better.

Things got a little awkward at that point, because I didn't know what to say next. So I did what nice Christian men and women do, I reached into my pocket, pulled out a twenty-dollar bill, and offered it to him so he could get something to eat. He looked at it, looked down at the ground, and then he said, "I think I'd rather talk for a little while if that's okay with you?" Well, I wasn't prepared for that. But I nodded my head in agreement and took a seat on the ground beside him.

He began telling me about his family. He had been married, but his wife left him for reasons he didn't disclose. He had two kids, a boy and a girl, but he only kept in touch with his son. By "kept in touch" he meant they talked once a year, but he felt like his son was ashamed of him. He didn't say much about his daughter. Only that she was beautiful and that he hoped, "wherever she was," she was happy.

He admitted mistakes he had made, as if he thought of me as a priest. He told me he had been saved at a Billy Graham crusade several years before but had struggled with forgiving himself for things he had done. I told him I've struggled with that too. He cried a little. I cried a little. I never have met a more honest man.

I looked down at my watch and realized that what had felt like only fifteen minutes had actually been a couple of hours. I told him my sound check would be starting soon, and I needed to get on my way. I said that I'd like to give him tickets to the concert that night if he'd like them, and he said he wasn't sure if he could make it. I left them at will-call anyway, but no one ever came to pick them up. Again I offered him the twenty dollars, but again he refused it. He said he was grateful for the conversation. That it was exactly what he needed that morning.

What he really wanted from me was not my money. He wanted me to notice him. He wanted me to look him in the eye and affirm that he was a person who was worth something. It was obvious he needed money, but what he needed more was healing. Healing that only the power of God can bring. He needed to get in touch with God that day, and God chose to use me in that process. I'm so glad I stopped to meet that man. I still think about him often.

The truth is we pass by these folks every day on our way to work. Some hold signs that say WILL WORK FOR FOOD. We spot some trying to find a warm place to sleep on the city streets of our hometown. Some even show up at our churches asking for some sort of benevolence. Truthfully, we might not even know some of the people in our lives that are in need of healing in one form or another. But one thing is for sure, these beautiful, broken people are all around us. It seems as though it's these people Jesus loves spending time with. They seem to catch his eye. In Matthew 21:14, Jesus spots a few people in need. Then he begins to heal them.

Compassion in Chaos

Let's take a minute to make sure we see this movie-like story unfold. Jesus has just created a huge commotion by turning over the tables. Animals are scampering for cover. Money is scattered everywhere. Tables are broken. The courtyard is in disarray, and people are running away from Jesus as fast as they can. Chaos, confusion, and bewilderment abound. This kind of thing had never happened before. Who would dare to vandalize the temple?

In the midst of all the craziness, though, are some people who don't run from Jesus. They don't try to get away at all. In fact, in an odd turn of events, they actually come to Jesus. I don't know how they physically got inside the courtyard. Some of them couldn't walk. Some of them couldn't see. My mind wants to imagine Jesus taking each of them by the hand and helping them inside.

Why would everyone run from Jesus except these people? Maybe it's because they couldn't get away? Maybe they had nowhere to go? Possibly, but I think they knew something else. I think they knew Jesus was a healer. With his touch he healed a woman who had been hemorrhaging for twelve years. With his spit he healed a man who had been blind since birth. With his words from miles away he healed a servant on his deathbed, and with a loud, tear-filled shout, he raised a friend from the dead. When people had access to Jesus, things happened. Lives got changed. Hearts were transformed. The blind could see and the lame could walk.

I think several miracles are happening here. The first is that Jesus notices the people everyone else overlooked. He not only gives them his time and attention, he gives them what they have wanted their whole lives: healing. Healing from disadvantages they didn't ask for. Healing from brokenness that runs so deep there is no way to measure the extent of their pain. Healing from not being accepted in a society that thought brokenness was a sign of unpardoned sin and that asking for help was the ultimate form of laziness. Healing needed to happen in these people, but those in leadership were too busy to see this. They were so busy "working for God" that they missed an opportunity to serve, to love, to care for those in need.

Religious scholars debate about many things, but helping those in need is not one of them. Nearly everyone agrees that God cares greatly about the poor, the helpless, the down-and-outs, and the broken.

Even Bono agrees. At a presidential prayer breakfast several years ago, he said: "God is in the slums, in the cardboard boxes where the poor play house. God is in the silence of a mother who has infected her child with a virus that will end both their lives. God is in the cries heard under the rubble of war. God is in the debris of wasted opportunity and lives, and God is with us if we are with them."

God is with the poor and he "is with us if we are with them." Those are strong words from U2's lead singer. I think he is right. It makes me stop and ask, am I with the poor, hurting, helpless, and neglected? Is God with me? These are good questions for all of us to wrestle with.

Hanging Our Welcome Sign

Have you noticed in the Gospels that the religious leaders run far enough away from Jesus that they're no longer in the line of fire and fury, but they stay close enough to see what he is going to do next. They were always watching him. He always had them on their toes. But they had no idea what to do that day in the temple when he started healing people. They became furious. It incited their anger even further when they heard children singing songs about Jesus being the Savior. In their minds Jesus was a criminal, not a savior. A vandal, not the Messiah. The spawn of Satan, not the Son of God.

But with a children's choir as his worship team, broken tables serving as pews, and a group of people who seemed more like a burden than a blessing, Jesus decided to have church. The altar call was pretty simple. Does anyone have a need? Come on in. Does anyone desire a miracle? Step right up. Is there someone who wants to be healed? Simply come forward.

One thing is painfully obvious to me in this story. Either we can stand arrogant and proud and watch Jesus work miracles from afar, or we can admit our brokenness and our need for him and have him work the miracles on us. I think it really might be as simple as that. Those who came to him were healed; those who didn't, weren't.

Do we come to Jesus when we need help? Do we create environments at church, in our homes, at work, or in our relationships that welcome people as Jesus did?

Van Gogh's Church

A few months ago, Amy-Jo Girardier, the student minister for girls at my church, introduced me to a painting by Vincent van Gogh. It's called *Church at Auvers*. Van Gogh painted this particular piece toward the end of his life. As I began to learn more about the artist's story, this painting became increasingly interesting to me.

Apparently van Gogh was not always a notorious painter. Most of his life he was virtually unknown. Even though some of his paintings now carry a price tag of more than eighty-two million dollars, his work didn't become famous until after he passed away. He was a genius at creating art, but surprisingly he had other aspirations besides painting. He wanted to be a minister.

According to a recent article I read, from the time of his youth van Gogh wanted to be in the ministry. He took an entrance exam to the School of Theology in Amsterdam but was denied entrance. He then volunteered to move to an impoverished coal-mining town in south Belgium where preachers were usually sent as punishment.

> He preached and ministered to the sick, and also
> drew pictures of the miners and their families,
> who called him "Christ of the Coal Mines." The

evangelical committees were not as pleased. They
disagreed with van Gogh's lifestyle, which had
begun to take on a tone of martyrdom. They refused
to renew van Gogh's contract, and he was forced to
find another occupation.

Van Gogh lost his job as a minister because he was living
among the poor. He was poor. He sold most of his possessions and gave them to the community he ministered to. Most
of the compensation he received from his pastoral work, he
distributed among those in need. I know van Gogh wasn't
necessarily a saint and he certainly had his struggles, but it
seems as though he was trying to undo something Jesus would
have undone. He was making sure that people in need were
not neglected. Nevertheless, the church didn't see it that way,
and they fired him. In light of his conflicts with the religious
leaders, it's interesting to look more closely at his *Church at
Auvers* painting.

Please Google this painting and look at it while I describe it
to you. It's a dark painting. I'm intrigued by it, but my instincts
don't like what I see. First, light seems to be all around the
church, but no light can be seen in the church. Is it possible
that van Gogh painted it this way as a statement about the
church? In his experience, the light of Jesus that the church
leaders claimed to promote and provide was not actually found
at all in the church he knew. He was asked to leave an impoverished community because his actions were unbecoming of a
minister. Maybe he was just trying to be a light the way Jesus

tells us to: "In the same way, let your light shine before others, that they may see your good deeds and glorify your Father in heaven" (Matt. 5:16). The light of God should shine through us to others. I wonder if van Gogh resented the fact that his light was taken away from that small mining community.

Secondly, can you see that two paths seemingly lead to the church but never actually make it there? Where are those paths going, and why don't they lead to an entrance of the church? Why is the path well worn if it leads to nowhere? There's someone actually on the path, but where is she going? Activity is happening around the church but not in it. I keep coming back to that point. People are trying to find a way inside to where they are told the truth is, but how do they get in?

Third, there is no door. This is the most disturbing part of the painting. There is no way to get inside the church. How can light get in if no one or no thing can get in? I realize this is speculation and has been in debate for a while now, but what if van Gogh was painting his experience with the church? What if he saw a beautiful building that didn't have the light of Jesus inside of it at all? What if, in van Gogh's mind, the church had been established to do something it wasn't doing? What if, in his experience, the church provided no doors to God, only walls?

If you were to paint a picture of your church, would it be a church with no doors? Would it be a place with no signs of life? Would it be a building where the light of Jesus never shines in through the windows and out into the world? Would it represent an establishment where no one is welcome? In all honesty I think that might describe some churches in North America.

In most of our churches we have a list of things you must do before we'll let you come inside. We have a "you need to get cleaned up before you come to Jesus" mentality. I just don't see Jesus actually asking people to get cleaned up before they come to him. I do, however, read several times throughout Scripture where Jesus invites criminals, prostitutes, thieves, and liars to follow him, and to some he even says, "You'll be with me in heaven today" (Luke 23:43).

I think van Gogh might have been saying the same thing through his painting that Jesus was saying through his actions in the courtyard that day. As Jesus-followers, we should be doors that lead people to Jesus, not walls that keep people from him. Jesus saw people in need and became a passageway to healing and restoration. He used his divine powers to help those in need, not to neglect them.

Am I neglecting someone in need right now? Are there ways I could be showing the love of God to someone? Am I choosing to be a wall instead of a doorway to God? I'm asking myself these questions right now. I realize that caring for people in need can be a thankless job. I know sometimes it's dirty, daunting, and difficult work. So many people need help and there's just one me. There is only one you. So much work needs to be done that at times it seems insurmountable. However, I'm reminded of Mother Teresa's words via Andy Stanley. She said, "Do for one what you wish you could do for everyone."

Your Church

Does your church care for people in need? Do you care for people in need? Sometimes it's as simple as praying and asking God to reveal to you people who are in need, and then doing your best to help them. Sometimes you donate time and money to causes you are passionate about. There are people in need everywhere. Everywhere you look, some person is physically, mentally, and spiritually in trouble.

Besides the fact that it is a biblical responsibility to take care of the "blind and crippled" in our world, can we not remember when we were spiritually blind to the truth of God's word? Can't we remember when we were crippled in our own sin? Do we remember when we were incapable of "pulling yourself up by your bootstraps," as Eugene Peterson says in Psalm 49 in *The Message*? Can we remember at some point standing at the proverbial gates of life, hoping for healing from the spiritual handicaps in our lives? All of us who are believers have been there. We've all been helpless. That's the point of a Savior. We can't save ourselves. Only God, through his Son Jesus, can do that. If God used someone in our lives to invite us to come to him, as broken, sinful, and dirty as some of us were, don't you think he might want to use us to invite others to him as well?

What if we were doors for others to get to God instead of walls to keep them away?

Lord I want to care about the things you care about. I know you want to help people in need. Help me love them like you love them. Amen.

CHAPTER FOUR

Hypocrisy

"The single greatest cause of atheism in the world today is Christians who acknowledge Jesus with their lips, then walk out the door, and deny Him by their lifestyle. That is what an unbelieving world simply finds unbelievable."

—Brennan Manning

If I had a nickel for every time I've had conversations with people about hypocrisy in the church, well, I'd have a lot of nickels. I've heard too many heartbreaking stories about how someone said one thing and then did another. I've heard this word *hypocrisy* related to why some churches split or why a pastor suddenly resigns. I've seen this word show up in discussions about divorce, scandal, and in some cases even criminal activity.

I don't like this word. I don't like the way it's sometimes used to describe the church or the followers of Jesus. I don't like it when it describes me. But the truth is, this was a real problem for the faith leaders in Jesus' day, and it's a problem for the church now.

While growing up, I can remember hearing several witty comebacks to people who accused Christians of being hypocritical and cited this as a reason for not going to church. They were catchy phrases such as, "Hypocrites are everywhere. You can go either to heaven or to hell with them. It's your choice." Or there was this popular one: "There are hypocrites at Walmart, and that doesn't stop you from going there."

But I have to be honest with you, I didn't really like those comments then, and I really don't care for them now. It's too blasé an approach to such a deep-rooted and emotion-filled discussion. Sometimes people aren't just using the "hypocrite speech" as an excuse for not coming to church. Sometimes I believe they're actually trying to tell us something deeper.

Maybe it's their way of telling us that something or someone in the church hurt them. Maybe they didn't understand something. Maybe they just want us to listen to them. Their complaint about hypocrites isn't an opportunity for us to quote bumper-sticker theology. It's a chance to start a conversation. It's a chance to be honest. It's a chance to apologize. We have the opportunity to let people know that the substance of Christianity isn't based on what Christians do but on what Christ did. It's a chance to point to the person of Jesus and his life.

And maybe, just maybe, with a closer investigation of the Scriptures, we might find that if we can all stop looking horizontally at people but rather look vertically to Jesus for our standard, we'd find exactly what we were looking for all along: a Savior.

But make no mistake, hypocrisy is one of the top reasons why people won't listen to Christians when we talk about Jesus or the church. As my pastor often says, "People aren't mad at Christians because we're too much like Jesus. They're mad because we aren't like him enough."

I've found that when we are discussing the word *hypocrite* with a friend or neighbor, it's important that we define it. Hypocrites aren't people who made a mistake once or twice. They aren't people who accidentally sinned or hurt someone's feelings. Hypocrites are people whose actions contradict their stated beliefs. In essence, they say one thing and do another on a consistent basis. Hypocrites are people who have two faces, one in public, one in private. They are actors. Phonies. Frauds. Pretenders.

I believe this is one of the reasons Jesus was so upset when he rushed into the temple and overturned the tables. The religious leaders claimed they were representing moral uprightness, holiness, mercy, justice, and kindness. Instead, they really represented greed, selfish ambition, dishonesty, and moral corruption, which made them the exact opposite of Jesus. They were hypocrites.

The Fruitless Fig Tree

I also believe hypocrisy is what made Jesus angry just a few hours later when he saw a fig tree with no figs. Matthew 21:18–20 tells us that story.

> Early in the morning, as Jesus was on his way back to the city, he was hungry. Seeing a fig tree by the road, he went up to it but found nothing on it except leaves. Then he said to it, "May you never bear fruit again!" Immediately the tree withered. When the disciples saw this, they were amazed. "How did the fig tree wither so quickly?" they asked.

When Jesus finished healing people in the temple courtyard, he decided to spend the night outside the city, perhaps because the religious leaders were furious with him. Jesus knew it was just a matter of time before they would arrest him, imprison him, and eventually murder him. However, Jesus was not finished undoing things. He saw another opportunity to teach his disciples about the hypocrisy that some of the religious community were displaying. This fig tree was the perfect opportunity.

When Jesus taught, he often used symbols to illustrate his point. He used sheep to teach about his never-ending pursuit of us. He said he would leave ninety-nine sheep that were doing well to find one that had lost its way (Luke 15:3–7). He used mustard seeds to show what a little bit of faith can do when it matures and grows (Matt. 13:31–32). Here Jesus uses a fig tree to teach us about hypocrisy.

Let me confess that I didn't know much about fig trees when I first read this passage. So I did a little research. Here are a few interesting facts. Fig trees can get as tall as twenty feet. They are great for shade because of their broad, wide leaves. The presence of a fig tree was a symbol of blessing and prosperity; likewise, the absence of a fig tree in the holy land was a symbol of judgment and deprivation. I also learned that they produce fruit before they produce leaves. When leaves were found on a fig tree, you could assume it also had fruit. That is, if it was healthy. So when Jesus saw a fig tree whose leaves were full, he thought it would have fruit on it. Unfortunately he found only leaves.

Many scholars believe this fig tree provided the perfect metaphor for the nation of Israel at that time, just as it did for a host of prophets before Jesus. In our Lord's time, Israel had become a fig tree with lots of leaves and no fruit. Much like the leaves, their speech was attractive and impressive. Their ceremonies and rituals boasted of a real and vibrant faith. They could be heard saying all the right things. They could be seen doing all the right things. From a distance they had all the promise of a healthy fig tree. It seemed as though they had a surrendered life that would bear fruit for God. Closer inspection, however, revealed that their tree was barren. There were no signs of fruit. There wasn't even one little fig on that tree. That tree was all leaves and no fruit—the essence of hypocrisy.

The Bible actually talks a lot about fruit on trees and vines. In John 15 Jesus shifts the metaphor from figs to grapes and tells us that God is constantly cutting off branches that don't bear fruit. It also says he's pruning the branches that are bearing fruit so that they can produce more. It seems as though it's all about the fruit! One of the most powerful moments of this chapter comes in verse 4. "Remain in me, as I also remain in you," Jesus tells his men. "No branch can bear fruit by itself; it must remain in the vine. Neither can you bear fruit unless you remain in me."

What Jesus teaches us here about grapevines is equally true for any fruit-bearing plant. If a tree is not growing fruit, it is somehow disconnected from its source of life. If we are not producing fruit, it's because we are disconnected from God. Spiritual fruit is the product of a relationship with God that is alive and well. It is proof that God is working in and through us. It's the evidence that we have been connected to the source of everlasting life.

A healthy Christian who looks back over his or her life will probably see patterns of obedience, sacrifice, and worship to God. They will see time spent with people in need, money given to build the kingdom of God, and love directed at God and their neighbor. All of these things have proven to be a great environment in which the tree of one's life can grow and bear fruit.

Producing fruit is not easy. It's not something that happens overnight. It's not something you can do on your own. However, bearing fruit is good. It does your heart good. It does those around you good. It does the kingdom of God good. Fruit is one of the goals of the Christian life. Remember the lesson of the fig tree. A Christian with no spiritual fruit is a worthless Christian.

Can you see why Jesus was so angry? The nation of Israel, God's chosen people, had become just like that fig tree. All leaves, no fruit. They were an empty display of what a God-follower should look like. God expected fruit from their lives, but they were producing only leaves. Appearance was more important to them than reality. They were hypocrites. Jesus came to undo hypocrisy.

Stinging Rebukes from Jesus

Nowhere does Jesus upbraid the Pharisees' hypocrisy more sharply than in Matthew 23. Over and over he calls them hypocrites. Typical of that harsh chapter are Jesus' words in verses 27 and 28: "Woe to you, scribes and Pharisees, hypocrites! For you are like whitewashed tombs, which outwardly appear beautiful, but within are full of dead people's bones and all uncleanness. So you also outwardly appear righteous to others, but within you are full of hypocrisy and lawlessness" (ESV).

This is the tone of someone who is completely fed up with hypocrisy and with the damage it does to people's perception of God. Remember a hypocrite is someone who acts in contradiction to their stated beliefs. They say one thing but then do another.

Did you know that the word *hypocrite* or some version of it is used seventeen times in the New Testament? Here are a few examples of Jesus using *hypocrite* to describe the actions of the Pharisees.

- Giving to the poor to be recognized by others (Matt. 6:2)
- Praying in public to be recognized as one of God's chosen (Matt. 23:14)
- Letting everybody know you are fasting to get recognition by others (Matt. 6:16)
- Complaining about others' behavior when yours is even worse (Matt. 7:5)
- Pretending to honor God through lip service only (Mark 7:6)
- Testing other people to try to make yourself look superior (Mark 12:15)
- Keeping seekers from knowing God (Matt. 23:13)
- Repressing the poor and widows (Matt. 23:14)
- Tithing (giving to the church), but neglecting justice and mercy (Matt. 23:23)
- Doing everything for show, while really being self-indulgent and unrighteous (Matt. 23:25) (Excerpts from a list in http://www.godandscience.org/apologetics/why_are_christians_hypocrites.html.)

Not an impressive résumé, huh? Would we want any of these things written about us? Would we want this epitaph displayed on our tombstone?

> **Here lies**
> _____
>
> **the hypocrite.**
> **He acted like he**
> **was honoring God,**
> **but his life never really**
> **brought glory to the Lord's name.**

Sometimes I wonder if this might be an accurate description of our lives. We know how to pretend. Some of the best pretenders I know are in church. I'm one of them. I've been guilty of pretending to be better than I really am. I've pretended that I know more than I actually do. I've pretended that I am concerned about the poor when five minutes earlier I just passed by several people who needed a meal.

Homeless in Nashville

I really didn't want to include this next story, but in the interest of trying not to be a hypocrite and sounding like I've got it all together, I decided I needed to.

I remember that I was participating in GMA (Gospel Music Association) week in Nashville. This is a week that celebrates and promotes Christian music from artists all over the world. Several media outlets are present, recording audio and video for their radio and television stations. For artists this means you are usually up way too early, doing live radio interviews. The early ones are always for the East Coast stations. We want to hit the heaviest listening time. In radio that's known as drive time.

Five A.M. that day was our first interview. That means we had to be there, ready to start the interview at five. That's pretty much the middle of the night for a musician. We knew it was important, though, so all of us took these interview opportunities and were glad that someone—anyone—wanted to talk with us about our music.

It was early April. It was cold. The streets around the hotel where the interviews were held were home to lots of people without homes. Grates on the sidewalks were hot air vents. People who were cold would sleep on these vents and find a little bit of warmth to keep from freezing in Nashville's cold night air.

On my way into the interview, I passed by four or five people lying on those grates in the middle of the sidewalk. They were just waking up. As I walked by, I wondered if they were hungry. I wondered if they had slept there all night. Or every night. I wondered what their names were and what had happened to them that they were without a home. It bothered me. But I hurried into the hotel, put a smile on my face, and began greeting the radio personalities who were gracious enough to play our music.

We had a ton of interviews that day, so the four of us in FFH (Far From Home) split up so we could cover more ground. I was flying solo, something that didn't happen too often. When the first interview started, we talked a little about new music and what was happening on the road. Then we segued to the next topic of conversation. They asked me a question that stopped me in my tracks. "Michael," the interviewer focused on me. "What do you think Jesus would do if he were walking the streets of Nashville today?"

For a few seconds I sat there stunned. When you're live on the radio, you try to avoid dead space at all costs. Silence is awful for radio. But I was trying to resist saying what was really on my mind. Finally the pressure of needing to say something forced it out of me. Here's what I said, as best as I remember it.

> Uhh. Hmmm. That's a tough one. I guess I honestly don't feel like I'm qualified to answer that question. The reason why is because I stepped over several homeless people in order to come in here and do this interview. You asked me what Jesus would do if he were walking the streets today? Well, if I'm answering with integrity, I must tell you that I think Jesus would have stopped and fed those people breakfast instead of rushing into this hotel to talk about his new record.

Once again we had silence. Now they were stunned. Frozen. Shocked. Finally, by a miracle of God, they somehow transitioned us to a break and then quickly thanked me for coming in that day and spending a few minutes with them. I had confessed my own hypocrisy live on the radio to who knows how many people on the East Coast. But what I had said on the air was true. I couldn't pretend to be someone I wasn't. I was tired of pretending.

Because I was so bothered that I had not fed these men and women on the streets, I went out and bought McDonald's biscuits for everyone I could find that I had passed by earlier that morning. I may not have done the right thing to start with, but I tried my best to make up for it now.

One man excitedly took a biscuit and told me that most Christians were too busy during GMA week to stop and talk to them, much less feed them. I was one of those people. All of this reminded me that it's never too late to do the right thing. If you feel you have been a hypocrite in certain areas of your life, do your best to ask for forgiveness, correct the issue, and try not to do it again. None of us are perfect, but we can always try to do the right thing.

A Truly Good Man

In concluding this chapter, I want to leave you with a story about someone who wasn't a hypocrite. Let me offer you a better challenge than just saying, "Don't be a hypocrite." I want to tell you about someone whose life was full of spiritual fruit. Someone whose stated beliefs and actions existed in harmony with each other. Someone who had leaves and fruit. Someone who was the real deal. That person was my wife's grandpa, Leo Chism.

Mr. Chism was a good man. I've known the Chism family for more than fifteen years now, and I've never heard a bad comment about the man. He was a man of integrity. I've been privy to countless stories about how he would stand up for what was right, even if he was the only one brave enough to do so.

Leo Chism was a hard worker. Sometimes during Christmas, when the family is telling stories about him, I'll hear about how he could outwork anyone, even as he grew older. He was a model husband and selfless father of three. I recall my father-in-law, Tom, telling me a story about how much he wanted a baseball glove when he was a boy. The family didn't have a lot of extra money at that time, so buying a baseball glove would constitute a major financial sacrifice for the whole family. But that was a sacrifice Leo Chism was willing to make. The family isn't sure just how long this actually took to accomplish, but Leo skipped lunch every day for a certain period of time. He did this so he could save every penny and eventually buy Tom his first baseball glove.

I've been fortunate to have a good relationship with my father-in-law. One day while we were at his house in Oklahoma, Tom said he had something he wanted to show me. When I asked him what it was, he told me it was a letter he wrote to his dad, Leo, just a short time before he passed away. Tom wanted to make sure his dad knew how much he loved him. He wanted him to know he was grateful for the sacrifices he had made for their family. Tom has been gracious enough to allow me to include this letter in its entirety in this book.

Dad,
I'm just reflecting on a few things today and I want you to
know the impact you have had on my life.
When I was a little boy, you provided me with
everything I needed and more. When I was scared,

all my fear went away when you got there. Dad could make everything alright. When I needed help, all I had to do was ask and you were there. When I needed to be disciplined, you did that too. You corrected me because you loved me. Every day of my life I have known that you loved me unconditionally. We had a happy home.

When I was old enough to start learning who God was, he seemed to be a lot like my dad. They said God loved us unconditionally, provided for our needs, that he would fight our battles for us and correct us when we are wrong because he loves us.

As I got older, I realized that what I saw in your life were the characteristics of God. It was only natural for me to love God, because I loved my dad and they were very similar in my eyes. I believe that the nearest I will ever come to seeing "the face of God" in this life, is in the example I have seen in your life.

One of the greatest blessings in this life, for me, is the privilege of being your son. Hopefully someday I can pass on some of your character to Jeff and Keely.

There will come a day when we will part for the last time in this life. When that time comes, because of the example you have set for me and countless others, I can take you by the hand and simply say, "See ya later, Dad," and know beyond the shadow of a doubt that I will.

I love you, Dad, for all you have done.

Your son,
Tom

I've read this letter at least a hundred times and I still get teary when I read the opening lines. Can you feel the impact Mr. Chism made on Tom? Can you sense the depth of love in their relationship? "I believe that the nearest I will ever come to seeing 'the face of God' in this life, is in the example I have seen in your life." What father wouldn't want this said about him? What son wouldn't want to have such a father?

Leo Chism was a hero. He made an extraordinary impact on his family because he loved them well. Their testimonies are evidence of the fruit in his life. The whole family has been spiritually affected for good by this man. Generation after generation will know who God is, at least in part, because of his life.

I can still hear Mrs. Chism, his wife, talk about him. Several years after he had passed away she began to dream about meeting him in heaven. Her health was declining, and we knew heaven was a reality she would soon experience. With a smile as big as Texas on her face, she would regularly tell the family about her beautiful recurring dream. "He looked young and handsome! He told me he had been waiting for me all these years. He took my hand and began walking me down the streets of heaven," she would beam. Then she would exclaim, "Boy, I sure do miss him!"

I have no doubt in my mind that Mr. Chism was a hero to her too! She longed for the day she would be next to him again. Why? Because he loved God, and her, and his family with all he had, and he showed it by the way he lived. It wasn't easy. It wasn't perfect. It wasn't televised so everyone could see what an unbelievable person he was. He didn't have a million fans on Facebook or multitudes of Twitter followers. As far as I know, he never accepted the Dad of the Year award. He simply did what was right. His tree was healthy. He had both leaves and fruit.

What does your tree look like? Does it have fruit and leaves on it? If Jesus were to inspect your tree, would he find fruit and bless it?

You know, our Maker is inspecting our lives. He's looking to see if our stated beliefs and our actions are the same. If we are believers, he wants to see fruit. He wants to see the evidence that we are who we say we are.

For Leo Chism this expectation was a no-brainer. When the test was given, he passed with flying colors.

May it be the same with us. Let's help Jesus undo the hypocrisy in our lives.

CHAPTER FIVE

Impotent Religion

Then Jesus said to the crowds and to his disciples, "The scribes and the Pharisees sit on Moses' seat, so do and observe whatever they tell you, but not the works they do. For they preach, but do not practice.

—Matthew 23:1–3 ESV

Yesterday I was reading a sermon that Martin Luther King Jr. preached in September of 1955 in Montgomery, Alabama. It was during the wake of a murder trial for the killers of a fourteen-year-old African American boy, who was lynched for allegedly whistling at a white woman. The two men who committed this awful crime were released after only one hour of deliberation by the jury.

In light of this moment in history, King begins to talk about the difference between a religion that pleases God and one that doesn't. Read this riveting piece of his sermon.

> Jesus condemned this over-emphasis on the ceremonial, because he knew the ominous effects that it could lead to. He saw that it could be the springboard of a religion which substitutes emotions for morals. This is what we are seeing in the world today—countless millions of people worshiping Christ emotionally but not morally. Great imperialistic powers, like Britain, France, and Holland, which have trodden and crushed Africa and Asia with the "iron feet of oppression," worship Christ. The white men who lynch Negroes worship Christ. That jury in Mississippi, which a few days ago in the Emmett Till case freed two white men from what might be considered one of the most brutal and inhuman crimes of the twentieth century, worships Christ. The perpetrators of many of the greatest evils in our society worships Christ. These people, like the Pharisee, go to church regularly, pay their tithes and offerings, and observe religiously the various ceremonial requirements. The trouble with these people, however, is that they worship Christ emotionally and not morally. They cast his ethical and moral insights behind the gushing smoke of emotional adoration and ceremonial piety.

To those who follow such a religion, we can [hear] God saying through the prophets, "Get out of my face. Your incense is an abomination unto me, your feast days trouble me. When you spread forth your hands, I will hide my face. When you make your loud prayer, I will not hear. Your hands are full of blood." Again he says, "Take away from me the noise of thy songs, for I will not hear the melody of thy viols. But let judgment run down as waters and righteousness as a mighty stream." This is always God's response to those who make ceremonial piety a substitute for genuine religious living.

I wish I could have been there to hear that sermon in person. I get goose bumps from simply reading it. Dr. King was urging us to understand what God really wants out of our religious practices. If God isn't a part of those ceremonial acts, or if we offer them simply for show, they are not only worthless, they are intolerable. I've come to know this as impotent religion.

For God, but Apart from Him

Impotent religion is useless. It simply cannot produce life in us. It does not contain the spark of love that gives birth to authentic change. It cannot result in a new creation that desires to follow Jesus. It only wants to follow itself. This particular brand of religion is dangerous, for all too often it becomes the poster child for the Christian faith.

Impotent religion is when we do something for God apart from God.

Granted, this kind of religion is subtle. The seed is usually planted in the hearts of those who really want to make a difference in their world. Generally, these people are passionate and persuasive. They're unafraid of criticism and are seemingly immune to giving up. They would charge hell with a water pistol if they were asked to. These people are prayer warriors. They're Bible quoting, hungry feeding, church-toilet-cleaning, door-to-door evangelists. They use discipline, hard work, intellect, and sacrifice to accomplish the task of spreading the holy word.

Somewhere along the way, however, something begins to change. People who used to speak with love and gentleness become more critical. The beauty of a love story between God and his people slowly turns into the rules and regulations of religion. They begin evaluating your performance as a Christian. They measure how dedicated you are to God by what you do for him. If they're honest, they usually compare your dedication to God to theirs. They use phrases like, "Be careful, God is watching you," and, "If you're not afraid of God, then you don't know him." They use fear as their source of spiritual motivation and their performance for God as their ticket into heaven. They would never admit to this, but in many cases they think they can earn or at least keep their salvation by their works. Their hearts preach the fallacy that salvation by grace is for the less dedicated ones. They've simply lost their way.

No doubt, some will be tempted to put down the book down at this point. If you're like me, you begin to see the faces of people you know and respect who have some of the traits I've just mentioned. Let me make sure you understand what I am saying. Doing religious things for God is not bad. In fact, things like reading your Bible and taking care of widows, orphans, and the poor are good religious activities. Praying and worshiping God together as a community of believers are good religious pursuits. But sometimes our perspective on these things gets a little bit skewed.

Doing What God Says

The truth is that God is watching you, but it's because he loves you, not because he's running you down like a cop chasing a bank robber. We should fear God, but that's because he is all-powerful. A healthy fear of him is critical to maintaining a posture of humility before him. He is God and we are not. What we do for God will be judged by God. In the next life we will be held accountable for our actions in this life. Loving God requires action for God. John 14:15 says that if we love God, we'll keep his commands.

There is no way to get around the fact that devotion to God means doing what he says. In a society that doesn't understand or like authority, this is a tough sell. But doing what God says is always the right thing. It's a healthy thing. It's the only way to truly build the kingdom of God. But when we do things for God or in the name of God apart from God, our religion becomes ineffective. Even the most spiritual act is lifeless if

God is not a part of it. The Bible says this kind of religion is like "whitewashed tombs . . . full of dead people's bones" (Matt. 23:27 ESV). It does not possess the ability to create life.

Did you know that the majority of the restaurant industry hates lunchtime on Sundays? It's true. Recently I asked a server at a local restaurant why Sundays are such a bad day. His answer made me cringe. He said the church crowd is rude. They're demanding. They think they're the only table in the restaurant. They don't tip, or when they do, it's not anywhere close to twenty percent. They leave tracts that look like a one hundred dollar bill and then say something like "the truth on this paper is more important than money." As one server said, try giving that tract as payment to the electric company who sends its bill every month.

The gospel *is* more important than money. That's true. But Jesus never asked us to stiff waiters as a means of showing them The Way. How can we leave church, where we celebrate how good and generous God has been to us, and then be stingy and self-absorbed as soon as we leave? This is just one example of how we can do things in the name of God apart from God. Can we not present the gospel in a better way than tricking someone into it? Why would we insult someone in the name of Jesus? More importantly, is that the example Jesus gave us?

Jesus never tricked people into following him. He never insulted people so they would convert to Christianity. He certainly didn't see rudeness and self-centeredness as a strategy for evangelism. In fact, I believe Jesus teaches that our actions as believers are supposed to give a glimpse into the character of God. Even though we aren't perfect, who we are and what we do should be evidence of God's love and compassion. His justice and mercy. His truth and grace.

The Pharisee in All of Us

Impotent religion is alive in the modern-day Pharisee. Somehow that Pharisee in all of us can be deceived into thinking that doing things for God is the same as doing things with God. Over the years I've seen this kind of thinking hurt the Body of Christ. Even worse, I see young adults every week who are tired of being sold that kind of Christianity.

I have worked with college students and young adults since I was eighteen years old. If you want to know one of the reasons why the church has had a hard time reaching young adults in America, it is in the last part of Matthew 23:3 that we looked at earlier: "They preach, but do not practice." The younger generation is the most marketed-to or advertised-to generation ever on the planet. They receive constant impressions or messages that promise to create a change in their life if they would only buy this product or that.

- Drink this brand of beer, and watch how many beautiful women will want to hang out with you.
- Wear this kind of perfume, and guys will fall all over themselves asking you out.
- You are rich and successful if you own this car.
- Lose weight and buy these clothes. Then everyone will love you.

There is little-to-no accountability for the promises that are made in advertisements like these. Whether it's in a commercial, an ad in a magazine, or on a bumper sticker, people are being sold something all the time. Because of that, most of us have developed a radar for the truth. We have developed a radar for people who are being dishonest. This generation can spot a fraud a mile away. They're watching you and me to see if the God we talk about is real.

Whenever we tell people how important God is to us or we preach about the necessity of God in our lives but then don't practice those very things, we create skepticism and distrust. We begin construction on a bad reputation for the church and for God that may take years to destroy.

I hear about this kind of thing too often after worship at Kairos. Kairos is young-adult Bible study that I've been attending and leading worship at for nearly ten years. Kairos doesn't have any age restrictions, but most who attend are somewhere between the ages of eighteen and thirty-five. I love getting to know these young adults. They are fun and smart and have tons of passion for justice. But the conversation usually takes on a different and somewhat somber tone whenever we get to questions about church. Specifically growing up in church. Like clockwork some will say they have been disenchanted with church because of the bad Christian example that they've seen in someone they trusted.

My answer is the same every time. Sometimes people make mistakes. Many times, if given the chance, they would do things differently. I remind them that the challenge is for them to be the kind of Christian they wanted to see while they were growing up. That statement is usually met with a half-hearted smile and yeah-I-guess-you're-right kind of response. It breaks my heart. I'm not perfect. You're not perfect. None of us are perfect. But our world deserves a better brand of Christianity than that.

If Jesus would undo impotent religion, then what does the Bible say about healthy religion? Remember, religion is not necessarily a bad thing. In fact, I think Jesus supported religion when it was used in the right way. After all, Jesus said he didn't come to abolish the law but to fulfill it (Matt. 5:17). Jesus actually started the church (Matt. 16:18). He commanded his disciples to baptize and to teach people to do everything he said (Matt. 28:19–20). Jesus encouraged prayer, fasting, and giving to God. He supported several religious acts. This is what Kevin DeYoung says about Jesus and religion: "If religion is characterized by doctrine, commands, rituals, and structure, then Jesus is not your go-to guy for hating religion."

I think Kevin is right. Jesus didn't hate religion. He preached about the need for religion. He simply hated impotent religion. He hated religion that was just a show. He hated to see religious acts being done for God apart from God. Healthy religion should remind us of our dependence on God rather than our independence from him.

Pure Religion and Undefiled
So what kind of religion should we strive for? That's the question we all should be asking.

James gives us some insight into what religion should look like. While this is not necessarily an exhaustive list of dos and don'ts, James is very clear about what he thinks religion is all about: "Those who consider themselves religious and yet do not keep a tight rein on their tongues deceive themselves, and their religion is worthless. Religion that God our Father accepts as pure and faultless is this: to look after orphans and widows in their distress and to keep oneself from being polluted by the world" (Jas. 1:26–27).

James seems to be saying that one of the standards for a healthy religion is the ability to control our speech. "A tight rein on their tongues" is an equestrian term. Just as we need a bit and bridle to control a horse, even so, James says, we need to bridle our speech. What we say is a good indicator of the kind of religion that is in our hearts. If we are unruly when we speak, James says our religion is worthless.

This section of James applies to losing our temper and saying something out of anger. I know there have been times when I wish I could go back and undo what I said in a moment of anger. I have friends who often say they wish they could take back what they said to their kids when they were upset. Be careful what you say when you're mad. Even though the apologetic expression "I wish I could take it back" may provide some relief for the person you hurt, the truth is you can't take it back. Once it's out there, it's out there. The damage is done.

Tweeting the Latest Dirt

This truth also applies to things like gossip. Even this sin is one we try to spiritualize sometimes. Too often gossip comes in the form of a prayer request. Sometimes it's in a prayer-chain phone call in which someone gives far too much information about the person who needs prayer. It seems as though some folks want to spread the sordid story more than they want to pray for the person involved. This is gossip.

We say things about people behind their back that we would never say to their face. This is also gossip. This is one of the things God is undoing in me. I'm trying not to say anything about anyone that I wouldn't say to their face. I call this the Hush Principle. When I wonder if something is gossip or not, most of the time, I simply need to hush, because it probably is. I realize there may be situations where this rule might vary. Sometimes in a work relationship you may be trying to encourage someone and not degrade them. Sometimes in a friendship relationship the same exception might apply. But all in all, the Hush Principle has helped keep me from gossiping.

Twitter and Facebook are some of the places where I see Christians out of control with their tongues (or their thumbs). I am appalled at some of the things I read on social media. So many hurtful words get posted. So many character assaults on people. Sometimes I see downright attacks on so-called "friends." It seems that some people don't feel responsible for their words on social media. They seem to grow braver behind a computer or mobile phone.

Can I just stop here and say that social media is not the best place to confront another person. It's not the best place to air out someone else's dirty laundry. Seriously, if Jesus was one of your friends or followers on Facebook or Twitter and he read your words, would he like what you've said? Would he be proud to be your "friend"? Controlling your tongue also means controlling what you text.

Be careful what you say. So much damage can be done so quickly. Trust and love that may have taken years to build can be destroyed with just a few words. I often tell myself this ten-word slogan from James 1:19: "Quick to listen. Slow to speak. Slow to become angry." I encourage you to memorize this if you struggle with controlling your tongue.

Spotless in a Dirty World

The next verse gives us two examples of pure and faultless religion. Again this is not an in-depth look at everything required to have a healthy religion, but we are giving a rather cursory glance into two categories. The first is outward acts, and the second is the inward life.

James points to taking care of orphans and widows in their distress as an indicator that our religion is healthy. This is not a new theme in Scripture, but it is a necessary one. Jesus agreed with this kind of statement wholeheartedly. In Matthew 25:40 he even states that when we do something for the least of these, it's as if we are doing it for him. If taking care of people in need is not on our list of priorities, James says our religion is not pure.

He also says that we should keep ourselves from being polluted by the world. The idea that James is trying to convey here is that we should invest tremendous effort toward being spotless or without blemish in our hearts. When nobody is watching, we should do the right thing. In our relationships, we should live cleanly. At work we should endeavor to be as pure in our motives as a fresh winter snow. All of these serve as examples of not being polluted by the world. The world may be unclean or immoral, but we don't have to live that way. We are to stay untainted by the conduct of people who surround us. In fact, we are actually supposed to impact the world rather than the other way around.

I've often heard it said that when you turn on a light in a room, the light affects the whole room. It is the light that pushes back the darkness. As believers, we are that light. Wherever we go, it should get brighter. This is one of the ways we can tell if we are making an impact on others around us. Is there more light or less when we're around?

We are sure to experience difficulty in pursuing genuine, pure religion. I remember hearing pastor and author Rich Stevenson explain the differences between the broad road that leads to destruction and the narrow road that leads to life—the roads Jesus talked about in Matthew 7. Rich said that for years he had pictured two different and separate roads in his mind. It wasn't until he got older that he realized they are both the same road. They're just going in different directions. The narrow road is going against the traffic flow of the broad

road. This explains why it's so difficult for us to journey toward life. We're literally going against the current.

In trying to keep yourself pure, it is vitally important that you monitor what goes into your eyes, ears, and heart. Watching trashy shows on TV won't keep your mind clean. Looking at shady websites and claiming they're harmless won't make you more godly. Listening or spreading rumors or gossip will cloud your world like the Los Angeles smog. Those things are pollution. Rid yourself of them at all costs. God wants purity for our minds so that we can think clearly and righteously. Any kind of pollution that keeps us from hearing or seeing him clearly is something he would undo.

James paints a picture of acceptable religion. We should control our speech, take care of those in need, and keep ourselves from being polluted by the world.

Is the religion you practice acceptable to God? Does it have the ability to give life, or is it impotent? Religion isn't bad. Jesus said so. But we have to keep in mind that other people may view God in a healthy or unhealthy way based on how we live out or practice our religion. As a good friend told me yesterday, the only version of Jesus some people will ever see is the lives we live.

What kind of Jesus does your world see?

CHAPTER SIX

Empty Worship

These people honor me with their lips,
but their hearts are far from me.

—Matthew 15:8

I think Jesus would undo empty worship.

I believe he would undo meaningless praise. He would undo all the times when what we sing and what we mean are two different things. He would undo all the moments when our lips and our hearts go in separate directions. When our talk is different than our walk. I believe Jesus would undo empty worship.

It's apparent from Matthew 15:8 that it is possible to state one thing with our mouths but live something completely different with our lives. We can say all the right Christian catch-phrases, go perfectly through all the religious motions, mind our spiritual p's and q's, and our hearts still be far from God. God is not just after our words. He's after our hearts. The center of our being. Who we've been, who we are, and who we'll become. He wants the real person inside, not the imposter. He wants the real you. The right words without real honesty from your heart are lifeless. Barren. Meaningless. Empty.

Could you imagine giving a perfectly wrapped gift to someone, knowing all along that once they opened it they would find nothing inside? How awful would you feel if you watched someone excitedly open a gift bag that you knew had nothing in it?

When we offer our songs, sermons, conversations, or spiritual devotions to God with our lips but don't offer our hearts to him as well, we are giving him an empty gift. A present with no present inside. In essence we offer him nothing.

According to Matthew, the problem really lies within our hearts. It's our hearts that are far from Jesus. If we have an empty-praise problem, we really have an empty-heart problem. A heart that beats for something else or someone else cannot claim to be wholly God's.

Fans or Followers?

Is it possible that God has many fans but few followers?

A fan is someone who wears the team colors. They might have the latest team apparel. They could have some of the players memorized. They might even be able to tell you about the team and its history. But a fan never intends to set foot on the field and actually play the game. They are simply a spectator—someone who watches the game but doesn't participate in it.

We have fans and followers in our churches as well. Inside the church a fan is someone who is not deeply overwhelmed with the courageous love and compassion of God that willingly walks into the broken areas of our world and promises and delivers healing. A fan is someone who is not bent over in gratitude for the cascade of grace that pours out of the heavens onto the sin-soaked soil of our lives. A fan is someone who can't let their busy life be interrupted by prayer, worship, Bible reading, or serving God by serving others, because their time is too valuable to waste on such trivial things that someone else will eventually do. A fan is someone who talks the talk but never intends to walk the walk. A fan is someone who honors God with their lips but not with their heart.

On the contrary we can find true followers inside the church as well. A follower is someone who is so consumed with the goodness and mercy of God that it naturally spills out of their life and into the lives of those around them. A follower is someone who takes the time to ask God to meet with them long before they walk into a church building on Sunday morning. A follower says, "Not my will but yours be done" (Luke 22:42). A follower is someone who is willing to march in the bloodstained footsteps of Jesus to where the broken, weary, cowardly, hated, self-righteous, abused, hypocritical, ugly, and forgotten people are. A follower says, "I will deny myself, take up my cross, and follow Jesus on the road to heaven," knowing full well it might go through hell first.

The difference between a fan and a follower is what's found in their hearts. Jesus knew that wherever our hearts are, our minds and bodies are close behind. If he gets our heart, he gets all of us. Friends, God is a jealous God. He wants all of us.

Hearts Full of Praise

I remember a few years ago my family came to visit Keely and me. My parents, my sister, and two of my nieces jumped in a minivan and drove twelve hours from Tulsa, Oklahoma, to Franklin, Tennessee. I love it when my nieces come to visit. I try my best to spoil them. We stay up late, eat lots of candy and ice cream, drink way too much soda, and then I hand them back to my sister. I feel like it's payback for years of teasing and torture from my older sister.

Once they arrived, we decided to get something to eat. I jumped in the driver's seat and off we went to a little diner near our house. Somewhere along the way, I heard Rachel's sweet little voice coming from the back seat.

> If you're happy and you know it, say amen. AMEN!
> If you're happy and you know it, say amen. AMEN!
> If you're happy and you know it, then your life will
>   surely show it.
> If you're happy and you know it, say amen. AMEN!

Needless to say, the whole van jumped in and was singing along. We all said AMEN as loud as we could! It didn't stop there, though. She kept singing.

If you're happy and you know it, clap your hands.
    CLAP CLAP!
If you're happy and you know it, clap your hands.
    CLAP CLAP!
If you're happy and you know it, then your life will
surely show it.
If you're happy and you know it, clap your hands.
    CLAP CLAP!

She went through all one hundred fifty-seven verses of that song. We were saying amen, clapping our hands, stomping our feet, bobbing our heads, and trying to turn around. That minivan was rocking with a children's praise song, and it was beautiful!

Until after the singing stopped, it didn't dawn on me what my niece was actually doing in the van that day.

She was leading our entire family in worship!

When I first realized what had happened, I was honestly a little frustrated, because for the last several years I have done my best to figure out how to lead people in worship. Now, my seven-year-old niece comes along and does it effortlessly. I think I know why. It may sound a bit trite at first, but I believe there's something deeper here.

The reason Rachel was able to lead our family in worship is because she was happy and she knew it. The lyric she was singing matched the life she was living. Her heart and her words were headed in the same direction. They were proclaiming the same thing.

Oh, how glorious the song must be to the ears of our great God when what we sing and what we live are the same thing. I imagine the heavens ringing out with beautiful chords our ears have never heard before. Oh, the magnificence of the angelic choir of our words and our actions blending together in perfect harmony!

Two Simple Tests

How do you know if your heart and lips are singing the same thing? It's easy to know what your lips are saying, because you can simply do a word audit. You can do this yourself, or you can have one of your friends who is around you all the time tell you what they hear you talking about most. Sometimes it's startling for people to find out what they say on a consistent basis. Most of the time, if the proof wasn't there, they wouldn't believe it.

However, it's a little harder to know what's in your heart, because that's something that, for the most part, only you and God know. No one else can tell you what's in your heart.

But there are ways *you* can know what's in your heart. Here's the test. It's simple. Jesus gives it to us in Matthew 6:21. "For where your treasure is, there your heart will be also."

What do you treasure? What means the most to you? What couldn't you live without? These are all road signs to where your heart is. If you love money, your heart will instinctively chase wealth. If you love your kids, your heart will do anything to protect them. If you love success, your heart will pursue every possible option to get ahead and climb the ladder. If you love God, ultimately your heart will be . . . broken.

Psalm 51:17 says this: "My sacrifice, O God, is a broken spirit; a broken and contrite heart you, God, will not despise." If you truly want to be a follower of Christ, if you really want to give your heart to God, if you desperately want your words and your heart to say the same thing, there is something you should know. He delights in the brokenness of our hearts.

What does that mean? Is God some demented spiritual force that revels in our pain? Is he some great cosmic comedian that rejoices at our suffering? No, not in the least little bit. In fact, nothing could be further from the truth.

When we read this Scripture, we have to remember that in the kingdom of God, broken things are beautiful things. It's one of those "upside-down" kingdom principles. At first glance these verses don't make any sense. Here are a couple of examples of upside-down kingdom principles.

The First Will Be Last
Sitting down, Jesus called the Twelve and said,
"Anyone who wants to be first must be the very last,
and the servant of all." (Mark 9:35)

Losing Life to Save It
For whoever wants to save their life will lose it, but
whoever loses their life for me will find it. (Matt. 16:25)

The Humble Will Be Exalted
For those who exalt themselves will be humbled,
and those who humble themselves will be exalted.
(Matt. 23:12)

These statements don't make sense in the world we live in. In the United States, the first shall be, well, first. He who gets to the front of the line is first, not last. Also, how can you save your life by losing it? We save our lives by climbing over everyone else. This is a dog-eat-dog world. We survive by being at the top of the food chain. We survive by winning, not by losing. And the humble will be exalted? Come on. The humble never get noticed. It's the arrogant that get exalted.

But that's only in the world we live in now. The rules of this earth are temporary. They won't last forever. However, God's ways and words are eternal. Read this beautiful passage from Isaiah 40:8: "The grass withers and the flowers fall, but the word of our God endures forever." God's word will last beyond tomorrow and the day after that. It will be around long after your last breath, and it will still be here when you stand in front of Jesus one day.

That's why as followers of Christ we can have confidence in Psalm 51:17. A broken or humble heart is actually the most spiritually healthy heart because it is in tune with God's. It most resembles his. God can use a broken heart. He can mold it and make it exactly what he wants. A broken heart in the Master's hands is a beautiful thing.

Remember it wasn't until Jesus broke the bread in Matthew 14:19 that the people could actually eat. The Bible says everyone ate until they were satisfied. I believe God wants to use us in great ways, but in order to do that, our hearts must be broken. Then God can use us as he sees fit. Once your heart is humbled or broken, then what?

A Love Story

I believe a heart fully committed to God needs to be broken so he can fill it with love. God doesn't want an empty heart. He wants a heart filled with the things that matter to him.

What really matters to God?

Love.

Matthew 22:37–40 says, "'Love the Lord your God with all your heart and with all your soul and with all your mind.' This is the first and greatest commandment. And the second is like it: 'Love your neighbor as yourself.' All the Law and the Prophets hang on these two commandments."

What does it mean to love with all your heart? This is something my grandpa taught me.

My grandfather was a good man, and he was a great grandpa. As a kid I would fight anyone who thought they had a better granddad than I did. I was lucky enough to grow up just a few miles away from my grandparents. Consequently, I was at their house often for a can of Coke and some of the homegrown peanuts my grandpa roasted at his house.

One of the things you need to know about my grandpa is that he was an amazing fisherman. Grandpa fished with famous people like Jimmy Houston, and he had a ton of stories about the fish he had caught. He told us about a sixteen-pound peacock bass from South America that he said put up an unbelievable fight and nearly chewed his lure into two separate pieces. He caught an enormous twenty-pound trout in Canada in very cold weather. It hung over the television set in the living room. He not only had pictures to back up these stories, he had mounted most of these fish and they were hanging on a wall somewhere in his house.

I loved it when Grandpa took me fishing. It seemed like he always knew where the fish were and, even better, he always knew how to catch them! But, if I'm being completely honest, I guess my favorite part of fishing with him wasn't actually fishing at all. It was our conversations on the way to the river. It was a little over an hour from Grandpa's house to Salisaw, Oklahoma, where his favorite boat ramp was. On the way there, we'd talk about everything from politics, to sports, to girls (or the lack of girls in my life as a teenager). But the last time Grandpa and I went fishing the whole conversation was about something more important to him: Grandma.

Grandma had Alzheimer's. Just in case you're not familiar with what that is, it's a degenerative disease that slowly takes away the mind of the person who has it. My grandma was totally dependent on Grandpa taking care of her, but she had no idea who he was. Let me give you a quick idea of what he did for her on a daily basis.

He would wake her up every morning and teach her how to eat breakfast. He would then help her go to the bathroom, help her shower and get dressed, and even sometimes drive her a few hours northeast of Tulsa to her childhood hometown in Arkansas, because she kept telling him she wanted to go "home." She hadn't lived there in more than sixty years, but Grandpa couldn't convince her of that, and he also couldn't tell her no. Sometimes several of those trips to Arkansas were made in a single week. He loved her too deeply to ever see her hurt.

He told me he was tucking her in bed one time, which by the way is such a beautiful picture to think of—Grandpa loving her enough to tuck her in bed every night. He said he made sure the pillows were fluffed just right and the covers were pulled up far enough. Then he got ready to get in on the other side of the bed.

Grandma blurted out, "What do you think you're doing?"

"I'm getting ready to go to bed," Grandpa said.

"Well, not in here you're not," she exclaimed.

"But I'm your husband and this is where I sleep," he said calmly.

"I ain't that kind of girl," she replied in a southern accent.

Grandpa smiled, nodded his head, grabbed his pillow and walked down the hallway to a spare bedroom just as he had done a thousand times before. At this point in the conversation, I interrupted him.

"Grandpa, have you ever thought about having a nurse come in to help take care of Grandma? This is a twenty-four-hour-a-day job, three hundred sixty-five days a year, and you've been doing this now for eight years. Have you ever thought about a nursing home for Grandma? Grandpa, you don't seem like you feel all that well either."

What I didn't know is that he felt awful. He had lost thirty pounds in the last six months, and his body was completely eaten up with cancer, but he had no idea what a mess he was in because he had spent all his time taking care of the woman he loved. That's when Grandpa interrupted me and held up his hand, which I'm pretty sure is the universal grandfatherly way of saying, "Hush."

Then what he said next I'll never forget. He looked me square in the eyes and with a shaky voice and a tear welling up in his eye he said, "Your grandmother took care of me for the first fifty years, and I'm gonna take care of her for the next fifty."

That statement rocked me. It's all I thought about while we were fishing that day. It's all I thought about on the way home. It's all I thought about for the next few weeks.

I was reminded of Grandpa's words to my grandma sixty something years ago on their wedding day. When he vowed that he would cherish her always, he meant it. When he promised to love her in sickness and in health, he meant it. When he said he would stay beside her for better or worse, 'til death do us part, he absolutely meant it. He had kept every word. Grandma died just a few months later, and less than a year after that, Grandpa followed her. Never have I witnessed a love story quite like that one.

My grandfather showed me what real love looked like. It's more than a word said with emotion. It's a word that's shown with devotion. It's a promise that's kept every day whether you feel like it or not. When we love like that, we begin to mirror the same kind of love that God has for us. Unconditional and unwavering.

How do we love God? I believe it's by offering him a humble heart that can be filled with love toward him and the people around us. When you're caring for an ailing wife or you're building an orphanage in Uganda, when you preach a sermon or hold babies in the nursery every Sunday, when you offer a kind word to someone even if they don't deserve it, you love God.

Loving God is always best shown in the lives we live. We then celebrate that in worship to him. When we sing of our love for the Lord, it already should have been expressed in various ways that week or we might be singing empty words. To sing or say words that we can't back up with the life we live means we are offering God empty worship. I believe that is something that Jesus would undo.

Maybe you have come to the end of this chapter and you need a starting point to get your words and your heart saying the same thing. I believe Psalm 51:10 is a good place to begin. This verse is written in such a way that it's easy to pray and easy to memorize. I would encourage you to memorize this verse and pray it often. Would you pray this verse with me?

"Create in me a pure heart, O God, and renew a steadfast spirit within me."

CHAPTER SEVEN

Pride

"If I had only one sermon to preach it would be a sermon against pride."

—Gilbert K. Chesterton

Pride has its grip on all of us. No matter how spiritually mature we might be, it's impossible to develop an immunity to pride.

Pride is listed as one of the seven deadly sins. In the New Testament it ranks among the top three. Pride is lethal. If it is not dealt with, it will destroy us and wreak havoc on those around us.

Pride is responsible for the first sin in the Garden of Eden where Adam and Eve want the knowledge of God but don't want to walk with him to get it. It shows up in young Joseph as he tells his older brothers about a dream in which they were all bowing down to him. According to Isaiah, pride is the reason Satan was cast out of heaven. To paraphrase John Milton's immortal words, Satan would rather have his own hell than God's heaven.

Pride single-handedly puffed up the Pharisees to the point that they couldn't recognize the Messiah after praying for him for many years. Pride dethroned kings like Nebuchadnezzar and Belshazzar. The Bible says that the wrong kind of pride brings disgrace and dishonor. It precedes a fall. God even says something drastic about it. He hates pride.

With a track record of destruction like this, why does pride still have such a high success rate? Should we not have this thing figured out by now? Shouldn't *I* have it figured out by now? I've personally had a front-row seat to the devastation this particular sin brings. Yet sometimes it still has its fingerprints on my heart. Why is pride so difficult to overcome?

Satan's Strategic Stealth

One of the reasons is that pride can be hidden so easily. It masquerades as strength. It disguises itself as independence. It uses the camouflage of intellect and bravery. It subtly boasts in its humility. All the while silently feeding on power and praise.

It also has the ability to morph and change at will. Even when we receive a compliment about our genuine humility, pride steps in and tells us to pat ourselves on the back because "somebody finally noticed."

Pride is not a respecter of persons. Whether you're a saint or a sinner, a thief or a theologian, pride is after you. If you don't think you have a problem with pride, it probably already has taken you captive.

Pride is like a Navy Seal that sneaks past your surveillance systems and covertly takes out your defenses. It avoids being detected because it is resourceful, smart, and well trained. It is an expert marksman, and its sights are set on one thing. You.

According to the dictionary, pride is an undue sense of our own superiority. It is the raising of ourselves above others. In *Mere Christianity*, C. S. Lewis said it this way: "A proud man is always looking down on things and people: and, of course, as long as you are looking down, you cannot see something that is above you." Then he warned, "As long as you are proud, you cannot know God." It is a warning worth heeding.

Lewis was right. The first thing pride wants to do is to blind us. It tries to impair our spiritual vision. It wants to distort how we see God and how we see others. Usually it begins by convincing us that God is not necessarily our master, but our consultant. He can give us advice when and if we need it. But, of course, as time goes on, we rarely need it. That is, unless we want to appear spiritual. Then we'll go through the necessary religious motions until we've satisfied our family, our peers, or our congregation.

Meanwhile, pride is blinding us.

After pride has convinced us to use God just as a consultant, it tries to make us believe that God is distant from us. He's the One who never seems to show up when we really need him. This, of course, leads us to take action and "do things on our own" (like we've been doing anyway, but pride doesn't let us see that). This is where the I-don't-need-God mantra starts. Of course, we'd never say that out loud. Only to ourselves. We become what Craig Groeschel calls "practical atheists." We believe God exists but live as though he doesn't. We forget that he controls every breath and every heartbeat. The sun rises and falls at his command. The waves of the sea go only as far as he tells them to go. But we can't see this.

Pride is blinding us.

As pride slinks into our hearts, we start to notice when we're honest that we only use the name of God in a negative way. "If God truly cared about me or this world, he would do this or that." In our minds and hearts, we begin using his name to precede curse words. We probably feel guilty about that, but eventually we reason that since God has been absent for a while, we're justified in our offense. This is a wrong-for-a-wrong kind of theology.

By this time we've completely forgotten what love and grace really are. When we see them in other people, we can easily explain away such goodness. "They don't really mean that," we may scoff. "They're just saying that to look impressive to others."

Of course, we do this because we are seeing everything through the lens of our own haughty spirit. We don't think gracious people mean their kind and loving words because *we* don't mean it when we talk that way. Once again, our pride doesn't let us see the truth.

Pride is blinding us.

Keeping Up the Image

We're probably still good at talking about love and grace, though. Pride always allows us to talk knowledgeably about things we don't really believe in. This is so we can keep our image intact, and that's of utmost importance.

Image is everything, and pride will do anything to protect it. Lie. Cheat. Steal. Sneak. These are things we never would have considered doing before pride put the veil over our eyes. But they are acceptable measures of action when our image is threatened.

By the way, we also probably still think we're doing *good* things. Right things. Godly things. We still know and quote Bible verses. We still attend church. We might even be on the church staff. But all the while a coup is rising up in our hearts to dethrone God and make us king. Pride wants nothing from us but everything. But it doesn't let us see that.

Pride is blinding us.

It also distorts how we see others. It falsely reminds us that God created us a little bit wiser, more disciplined, better look- ing, or far more dedicated than anyone else. Again we would never notice this happening in us unless we have people who are close to us who will tell us the truth. But, of course, if they did tell us the truth, in our mind they would be "judging us." Pride argues like a masterful lawyer in court. It has a countermove for every dispute that might expose its presence in our hearts.

Pride creates a false reality in which we are always the center. There's a reason why the letter *i* is in the middle of the word *pride*. When pride has a hold of us, we will always be the center of our own universe. We will also want to be the center of everyone else's.

It's common to hear the word *better* from someone who struggles with pride.

I'm better than this.

I'm better than her.

Why isn't my life better than his?

I deserve better.

But, of course, we probably will never see ourselves as someone who would say things like that. Why?

Pride is blinding us.

Pride will ruin both our relationship with God and our relationship with others. It will keep us from understanding how undeserving we are of God's forgiveness. That's one of the reasons we'll then have a hard time forgiving others. Pride wants justice, not forgiveness. Unless, of course, it's justice against us. Then we'll be in favor of forgiveness. Once again, we won't be able to see this clearly.

Pride is blinding us.

Going for the Glory

As pride steals into our souls, we'll wonder why people around us aren't more merciful to each other. We'll say things such as, "This world is going to hell in a handbasket." But we'll never see that with our pride we're helping to carry that handbasket. We won't be able to comprehend that we're really part of the problem, not the solution. This is because pride wants one thing above all else. Glory.

That's right. Pride is after personal glory. It wants us to lift our name above every other name. Above our friends. Above our family. Above our co-workers. Above God. All to give *us* glory. Every breath. Every step. Every day begins to be about our glory.

Can you imagine singing hymns and worship songs to yourself about your own glory?

"Praise ME from whom all blessings flow."

"How great I am, sing with me, how great I am."

Doesn't the very idea of that just make you sick? I hated actually typing those lyrics, much less singing them.

Can you imagine preaching or teaching that the Christian life is all about *your* glory?

"So, whether you eat or drink, or whatever you do, do all to the glory of YOURSELF."

"For all have sinned and fallen short of MY glory."

This kind of theology would be heresy in the church. However, when pride convinces us that our glory is more important than God's, in essence that's what we're doing. That's what we're preaching and singing. We are worshiping our name above all names. God hates pride because pride wants us to glorify ourselves instead of him.

Pride is destructive. It's selfish. It will blind us. It will do anything to stay alive in our hearts. So, how do we defeat pride?

Undoing Pride

If we can agree that pride is something Jesus would undo, what is our first step?

We need to ask God to remove our pride and replace it with humility.

Your knee-jerk response may be to assume that this is too elementary. You may be tempted at first to dismiss my suggestion. Understand that this is pride talking to you. It wants to blind you to the truth. Remember, it wants nothing to do with someone else's glory. It wants only yours. Push through the temptation to ignore this part of the chapter. Information about pride, without action, does nothing to kill it.

Pride will lead you to believe that, because you have read this far, you've done your good deed on this subject. But it's just trying to get you to destroy it tomorrow instead of today. Both of us know that if you wait, you probably won't do it tomorrow. Ask God to eliminate your pride now. He'll usually do that through the process of humbling you. Your prayer could be as simple as: "Lord, remove my pride. Amen."

I remember that when I was nineteen, a friend of mine asked how he could pray for me. I told him I wanted humility. Real humility. The kind I had seen in him and other leaders like him.

He then told me, "I'd never seek that for you. That's something you'll have to pray for yourself."

I asked him why.

He looked down at the ground. Then he smiled and said, "That kind of prayer is good to pray. It's right to pray. But God always answers that prayer. Usually it's in a way that brings discomfort and difficulty to your life. Pray that one on your own."

I didn't understand what he meant then. But after praying that prayer repeatedly for several weeks, I began to understand. Suffice it to say that God began removing the pride within me. He did that by taking away most of the things that gave me personal glory. When our glory becomes threatened, that's when our pride is exposed. When it is exposed, we must identify it. Then we must destroy it.

Embracing Humility

If pride was a poison, the antidote would be humility. Humility is a modest or low view of one's own importance. We have to take on this kind of posture if we seek to have a healthy relationship with God and others.

In a book titled *A World of Stories for Preachers and Teachers: And All Who Love Stories That Move and Challenge*, William J. Bausch recounts a story about the funeral customs of an Austrian royal family. The edited excerpt of that tale inserted below beautifully illustrates my point. Humility even applies to royals.

In Vienna, Austria, there is a church in which the former ruling family in Austria, the Hapsburgs, are buried. When royal funerals used to arrive, the mourners knocked at the door of the church to be allowed in. A priest inside would ask, "Who is it that desires admission here?" A guard would call out, "His apostolic majesty, the emperor." The priest would answer, "I don't know him." They would knock a second time, and again the priest would ask who was there. The funeral guard outside would announce, "The highest emperor." A second time the priest would say, "I don't know him." A third time they would knock on the door and the priest would ask, "Who is it?" The third time the answer would be, "A poor sinner, your brother." And the door would be opened wide. (326–327)

Every moment we are on this earth, we are to be about the business of bringing glory to God, not ourselves. As Christians, we don't come to God as kings and queens. We don't come to him as CEOs or senior pastors. We don't approach God as models or musicians. We come as sons and daughters who have been graced with a real relationship with God, our Father. We come as worshipers who are willing to exalt God above all other gods, including ourselves. We come to God saturated in sin, full of ourselves and self-righteous but asking for mercy and grace. God's love turns a slave into a son and an orphan into a daughter.

When we lose sight of those truths, however, we often come to God as the Pharisee did in Jesus' parable found in Luke 18:9–14:

To some who were confident of their own righteousness and looked down on everyone else, Jesus told this parable: "Two men went up to the

temple to pray, one a Pharisee and the other a
tax collector. The Pharisee stood by himself and
prayed: 'God, I thank you that I am not like other
people—robbers, evildoers, adulterers—or even
like this tax collector. I fast twice a week and give a
tenth of all I get.'

"But the tax collector stood at a distance. He
would not even look up to heaven, but beat his breast
and said, 'God, have mercy on me, a sinner.'

"I tell you that this man, rather than the other,
went home justified before God. For all those who
exalt themselves will be humbled, and those who
humble themselves will be exalted."

In this parable the Pharisee's pride was blinding him. He had
lost sight of the fact that the same grace that was extended to
the tax collector was extended to him as well. He couldn't see
that his prayer was offensive to God. He might as well have
been praying to himself. He and the tax collector were standing in the same line for mercy. But only one received it. The
tax collector.

A friend of mine who is an excellent Bible teacher often
says that he is just "one beggar telling other beggars where to
get bread." He understands that even with all the intellect he
possesses, he is in need of Jesus. We all need Jesus.

Humility denotes dependence on something greater than
itself. In Christianity it is the understanding that God is the
Great Giver of all we have. Whether it is the shoes on our

feet or the breath in our lungs, he provides it. Our lives are a humble response to him and his graciousness toward us.

Humility isn't perfection. It is honesty. It is engaging in the discipline of transparency when we would rather hide our imperfections and flaws. It is open to correction and rebuke. Even though reproof might be hard to swallow, we swallow it nonetheless. Remember what the proverbs teach us. It is the wise man who accepts correction (Prov. 15:31).

Humility has no regard for reputation or acclaim. Those who are humble seek to build up others instead of themselves. When they do receive glory, they quickly divert that attention to the One who deserves it. A humble man knows his place. It's not on a pedestal or a throne. It is kneeling before God's throne. He realizes the God of the Infinite is infinitely greater than himself (Mark 1:7).

Humility always seeks to serve. A humble person routinely says "you first." Humility doesn't demand to be served. That would contradict the example Jesus gave. Humility realizes that it really is "more blessed to give than receive" (Acts 20:35). It knows that, in actuality, the giving becomes part of the receiving. The approval we sense from God in giving is what we really want most.

Humility involves a deep awareness that we work in fields we do not own. We are stewards of what belongs to God. Even when we are tempted to grasp our possessions too tightly, humility reminds us that our hands are far better for holding on to God than to stuff (Luke 16:1–12).

A humble man is often silent. Even though he could "wax eloquent" about subjects he has studied and pondered, he listens. He knows God gave him two ears and one mouth for a reason. He listens more than he speaks (Jas. 1:19). Ironically this is usually the trait his friends admire most about him.

Humble people don't insult themselves in front of others to garner compliments or to pacify their insecurities. They do not indulge in this kind of false humility. It's simply a ploy to elicit praise (Col. 2:18).

Once again, C. S. Lewis states it so well in *Mere Christianity*. "True humility is not thinking less of yourself," he wrote. "It is thinking of yourself less."

A humble person knows that God "opposes the proud, but gives grace to the humble" (Jas. 4:6 ESV). The grace he receives from God is far more important to him than all the rubies, diamonds, and emeralds that pride could offer him.

A humble man doesn't compare himself with others but rather with what God has made him capable of. He only measures himself by what God has asked him to do and be. No more and no less (Gal. 6:4).

Humility scrubs the toilet.

Humility brings donuts to work without requiring a thank you.

Humility respects others, even when those "others" are his enemies.

Humility hurts.

It stings.

It bleeds.

Humility's Perfect Model

When it comes to true humility, our best example is Jesus. Have you ever really thought about the humility it required for Jesus to endure his arrest? The pain of his beatings? The punishment of the cross? His brutal death?

After he was arrested, Jesus would have received his punishment naked. Soldiers who were skilled in the art of punishment would have forced him to bend down with his hands and legs tied to a post coming out of the floor. The soldier would have then taken his whip with claws on the end of it and thrashed it against the body of Jesus. Each strike would have peeled flesh, bone, and blood from his torso.

With his body broken and bleeding, they strapped a cross to his back and made him carry it through town to humiliate him. He was walking to his own death site. People hurled insults at him. His body collapsed under the enormous weight of the cross. The Savior of the world fell to his knees. The King of kings bent down to pick up our cross.

Once Jesus made it to the execution site, the soldiers then nailed him to the cross. Two nails went into his wrists and one near his feet. Then they dropped the cross with Jesus nailed to it into a hole in the ground so the cross would stand upright. There our Savior would hang for the next six hours.

People mocked him. They scorned him and made fun of the claims he had made as a teacher. They taunted him as King of the Jews. They laughed at him, wondering how he could save mankind if he couldn't save himself. The Son of God, with all the power and might of heaven at his fingertips, chose to stay on that cross and die there.

He could have called the angels down to rescue him. He could have used his divine powers to free himself from the grip of the suffering and pain. He could have said, "Enough is enough," and all of creation would have been silenced. Instead he suffered a brutal death so we might have a shot at life. Real life. Abundant life. Eternal life.

I'm wondering how you and I can know and understand the brutality of the sacrifice of the cross and still remain prideful? How can we read about Jesus taking on the ultimate form of humility and still be infatuated with ourselves? How can we be conscious of the suffering of Jesus and then arrogantly live a self-centered life?

Plain and simple, it's because pride blinds us. We lose sight of the cross. We lose sight of his sacrifice. We lose sight of Jesus.

Pride is something that Jesus would undo in our lives. In my own prayer time I keep coming back to Psalm 139 and praying this psalm to God. Would you join me?

> *Search me, God, and know my heart; test me*
> *and know my anxious thoughts. See if there is*
> *any offensive way in me, and lead me in the way*
> *everlasting. (23–24)*

Even as I write this chapter, I am confronted with my own pride. When I set out to write this book, I had no idea how much

I would need to hear the things God is allowing me to write. I guess an author writes the things he needs to learn most.

Now, on to the next chapter.

Condemnation

*For God did not send his Son into the world
to condemn the world,
but to save the world through him.*

—John 3:17

It is with prayerful caution that I write this chapter. In and out of the church, this may be the most popular topic of conversation related to Christian behavior. I've seen people leave church and never come back because of it. I've seen church staff meetings turn into wrestling matches because of it. Some say it's unbiblical. Some say it's completely biblical. There are churches whose motto is to eradicate it, while other churches create a culture of it.

Why are we so confused about the subject of judging others?

Our churches are filled with people who either hate the idea of condemning others or wholeheartedly endorse it. We are terribly divided on this issue. Even as I write this chapter, I know the temptation is to choose sides. I don't like that. As believers in Jesus Christ, we're all on the same side as far as I'm concerned. However, I will do my best to unpack what I've learned, and hopefully some of my mistakes will provide you with information that is beneficial to you.

Let me first say that I deeply desire for you to hear Jesus speak in this chapter. I hope you feel God's love and affection for you as you read. I pray that those of us who need healing and restoration will receive it in Jesus' name. That those of us who need correction and discipline will receive it as well. I know the words *love* and *discipline* don't often flow well together. But I also believe that God's love is perfect. Even when it hurts, it's good. Please read this knowing my intent is to write with grace and care.

Judgmental Christians

Everybody's talking about it. Twitter tantrums, Facebook rants, and other online discussions can get pretty heated about it. Coffee shops, living rooms, and television programs are filled with it. It happens in hallways at work, in grocery store lines, and on street corners. Judgmental Christians are a hot topic.

Although it seems to be on the tip of everybody else's tongues, I haven't often heard this subject preached about in church. I mostly hear this topic talked about by church attendees rather than by church teachers or preachers.

Maybe that's why the subject often comes up in a negative connotation. Usually, the conversations are emotionally charged, and they regularly end up in dispute. As is true with most hot issues, two groups of people seem to be on opposing sides. For our purposes, we'll call them Group A and Group B.

Group A will say things like: "Can you believe they judged me like that? Who do they think they are?"

Why are they upset? Because they believe that judgment has been passed on them when they didn't think they deserved it. They feel as though their actions didn't warrant any kind of outside verdict. Some members of this group, in fact, feel as though their actions never warrant judgment. At no time should someone tell them that what they're doing is wrong, immoral, or ungodly. The exception might be something drastic, like murder. But, generally speaking, they are not for anyone but Jesus judging them. They believe that the only way you can possess the right to judge another is if you are perfect. God is the only One who is perfect, so he is the only One who can accurately judge. That is how Group A thinks and reacts.

Group B would say something like this: "Pointing out when people are wrong, either theologically or in behavior, is part of my Christian duty. Our culture is far too soft on this. If I don't tell them, who will?"

People who are *for* judgment usually don't use that word. Maybe it sounds too harsh. Maybe they don't think that's what it is. But they seldom use that word. Still, they genuinely feel an obligation to point out the flaws in others. Correcting others is as much of a responsibility as reading your Bible or saying your prayers. To avoid doing this would be to renounce the very principles of Scripture. To do that is unthinkable to them.

Both Group A and B feel as passionate about their positions on this subject as an Olympic athlete feels about holding up her national flag at the opening ceremonies. Heart pounding, face reddening, muscles clinching. This is serious. This is real. With all their hearts, both sides believe they are right.

So, who is right? How do we know which side to choose?

I believe that in some cases both of them are right. I also believe in some cases both of them are wrong.

This is a complex discussion and all of us know about too many instances where people have been hurt and embarrassed by someone who inappropriately judged them. For this, I am deeply sorry. I wish I could go back and enter the moment when you were wronged and change it. But I can't. Only Jesus can heal that wound, and I pray that he will. I know it has been said that "time heals all wounds." Whoever said that lied. Time *hides* all wounds. Jesus is the only One who heals them. I am praying that our Lord's healing washes over you as you read this.

With that said, I must add what I intend as constructive criticism of the position of Group A. A fatal flaw lurks in the argument that asks, "Who do they think they are? Nobody has the right to judge me." In their insistence on not judging someone, they themselves have judged. They are making a judgment when they say that someone has judged them. Maybe they have not intended to. Maybe they will wish to change their words once this point comes clear to them, but the hard truth is that the anti-judgers are judging. They have made a ruling about someone based on their actions. Any judgment they make on the ones they call judges defeats the purpose of their argument. You cannot pronounce judgment on someone in the name of not judging.

The Real Issue

Now let's address the real question.

Can we judge someone? Is it ever right? Dallas Willard has given us a beautiful perspective on this. (Honestly, I wish I could include the entire chapter from his book *The Divine Conspiracy*. It has been enormously helpful to me as I studied this topic.)

> A dentist may examine a patient's teeth and say, "I see you have not been brushing regularly. Your gums are receding, and there is a cavity over on the lower right side." When he does this, he is indeed judging the condition of the patient's teeth and gums and practice of dental hygiene. He is discerning, seeing, and saying what.it is. But he would not usually be thought of as condemning us or our gums and teeth. He is appraising their condition in distinction from other, more desirable conditions. (384–385)

In this example the dentist is simply doing what he or she gets paid to do. They are evaluating patients and helping them avoid problems that most certainly lie ahead for them without some kind of remedy. They are not condemning them. They are not hating them. They are not blasting them with irresponsible accusations. They are simply giving the facts in order to assist the patients with the problems inside their mouths. Most of us would agree that we must be willing to hear and act on what the dentist has to say if we want to make sure our teeth stay healthy.

Sometimes this is where we have major problems if we are in the dentist's shoes. Correcting someone is different from condemning someone. I don't intend to condone condemnation at all. In fact, it's flat out wrong. Condemnation is completely against the teachings of Jesus (more on that in a minute).

I am convinced, however, that there are times when it's necessary to help our Christian brothers and sisters return to a healthy, intimate relationship with both God and their community. Restoration is always the goal of correction or judgment. Our intent should never be to "straighten them out." It should never be to satisfy our need for control or order. Certainly, it should never be to saddle people with the weight of embarrassment for the sake of embarrassment alone. Our goal in the process of reproof should always be restoration, to bring the wayward back to the very table of grace from which we ourselves dine.

I should also note that if we are willing to judge or correct others, we should also be open to receiving judgment or correction ourselves. This street goes both ways. Many of us are far more comfortable correcting the faults of others than having our own straightened out. As mature believers, we must suppress the urge to fight back. We must welcome the discipline that makes us more able to surrender to Jesus and his teachings. If we are being reminded of his words and principles through the loving judgment or correction of another, we must embrace it.

As Dallas Willard states, correcting someone is reserved for those who first know all the facts. If we are tempted to correct someone based on speculative testimony and sparse evidence, we should be slow to start the process of correction. Other steps may need to be taken, but correction is not one of them. These decisions must be made carefully and prayerfully. Generally speaking, private conversations are the best and proper first step. Sometimes people are unaware of what they have done. By revealing this in private to them, we can save them from needless embarrassment. Hurting someone's reputation is not the goal of judgment. Restoration is.

Second, when correction is done, it is to be done in the spirit of *agape* love. This love is not based on passionate emotion but on unwavering devotion. It is the love that Jesus has for us. We must love as he did. This is where some confrontations may go awry. Sometimes we act more in the spirit of anger or fury. All hope is usually lost when our voice takes on an angry tone. I'm with Dallas when he said that he cannot trust himself to correct someone in this spirit. He'll leave the angry confrontations to Jesus.

Greater Than All Our Sins

Can you see how Group A can be wrong and right at the same time, though? As I pointed out earlier, you can't judge others in the name of not judging. However, the guidelines for necessary judgment or correction are not always followed lovingly and obediently. Sometimes those judgments, although much needed, feel more like condemnation. Sometimes they are condemnation. Jesus strictly prohibits this. This is something Jesus would undo.

If we fall into Group B, let's remind ourselves that condemnation is wrong. Regardless of our reputation or education, it's wrong. Even if our moral conduct is blameless and our attendance record at church is perfect, we are not free to condemn others. It's wrong. Condemnation isn't right, even if we ourselves have been wronged. None of us has the right to condemn someone else. John 3:17 points out that God didn't send Jesus into the world to condemn us but to save us. If Jesus doesn't stand in condemnation over someone, who are we to?

Romans 8:1–2 says, "Therefore, there is now no condemnation for those who are in Christ Jesus, because through Christ Jesus the law of the Spirit who gives life has set you free from the law of sin and death."

Those are the words of God through the apostle Paul. There is no condemnation for followers of Christ. We have been freed from the condemnation of our sin. To enforce this kind of judgment on someone would not only be unbiblical, it would be hateful.

Condemnation seeks to injure or harm. Its desire is to sentence someone to some degree of punishment so they can pay mentally, physically, or emotionally for what they have done. Such condemnation delights in saying, "Guilty as charged." In short, it requires recompense for sin.

This is the opposite of grace.

This is why Jesus was against it. He paid for our sins. Working for salvation would undermine the sacrifice of Jesus as if it were not enough. As if he was not enough. Grace reminds us that "if the Son sets you free, you will be free indeed" (John 8:36). Eugene Peterson calls it "aggressive forgiveness" (Rom. 5:20 MSG). Webster calls it "unmerited favor." I call it cause for celebration because without it I'd be lost. Hopeless. Condemned.

As believers in Christ, we must never forget this. Grace has changed our destiny. "By grace you have been saved" (Eph. 2:8). Our lives are soaked in grace! We must all stay constantly alert to this reality. **A heart full of grace would never offer a mouth full of condemnation.**

When we are conscious of this grace, we should desire to extend it to others as well. Our response should never be to sentence someone to punishment, but rather to lead them back to the gracious One. Can you imagine how much healing would take place if we were to offer grace-filled correction with the same passion that some of us extend hateful condemnation?

Condemnation is a burden we can't carry. It's a yoke we can't bear. Why would we force someone else to shoulder the load that only Jesus can carry? When we condemn others, we are going against all that Jesus taught and lived.

Better Than You

Condemnation is a product of self-righteousness, which is an exaggerated view of one's own virtuousness or rights. In order to condemn, one must have the right to do so. Self-righteousness helps us believe that we do have the right. Somewhere along the way, our egos have convinced us that who we are or what we've achieved makes us good. Or at least better than the next guy.

The assumption that we are better than others can be found in both the younger and older generations. Sometimes the younger generation assumes it's only found in the older one, but I know better. I have seen many self-righteous young adults. They were just proud about not being self-righteous. As Kevin DeYoung points out in his blog, some young adults might say, "I am not this. Therefore, because I am not this, I am better than you." Or, "I don't do this. Therefore, because I don't, I am better than you."

The arrogance of self-righteousness can be found in all humans. It shaped Jonah's attitude toward the Ninevites. It was in full bloom with the Pharisees and some of the religious leaders in the New Testament. Here's the hard truth. It's also found in us.

If we ever hope to correct someone who has lost his way, we must first correct the self-righteousness that leads us astray as well. The "plank in my eye" (Matt. 7:3) often keeps me from seeing correctly the speck in my friend's eye. We would do well to examine ourselves carefully before endeavoring to examine or judge others. I am not saying it can't or shouldn't be done. I'm simply saying it's best done by those who are close enough to Jesus to be reminded that, whatever wrong road someone has gone down, we are capable of walking down that same road and much worse. "There but for the grace of God go I" should be the refrain we utter in our hearts when we seek to correct others and help them find their way back to the Light.

Show Me the Way

A posture that is able to receive correction and instruction is equally important. Too many good men and women have hurt themselves and others because they simply would not listen to a corrective voice in their life.

I enjoy watching conspiracy theory movies once in a while. Recently, I watched one about JFK. In it they spent a great deal of time revealing some of the warnings the Secret Service had received about an attempt on the president's life. Those in charge of Kennedy's motorcade in Dallas that day assured everyone, including the president, that they had everything covered. Despite repeated attempts at getting those in charge to consider changing Kennedy's route, the motorcade pressed on. They did not listen. As Kennedy made his way into the final and most vulnerable turn of that route, gunshots rang out. President Kennedy was killed at the exact spot the Secret

Service was warned about. The movie posited that if they had listened, the president might still be alive today.

Now, I understand this was a conspiracy theory movie, and I have no intention of trying to prove or disprove the truth of this matter. I simply wanted to illustrate the importance of listening to the corrective voice of others. In matters that are legitimate, we should always be willing to hear the voice of correction. "Whoever heeds discipline shows the way to life" (Prov. 10:17a).

In essence, this proverb is telling us that if we really want to be successful at this thing called life, we have to listen to correction. There's no way around it.

I listened when my dad told me to stand up straight and look people in the eye when I talked to them. Apparently, I didn't come out of the womb knowing how to do this. Even though this wasn't necessarily natural for me at first, I listened to my dad and soon it became a habit. When I was starting my first business mowing lawns, an older gentleman told me he hired me, not because I was great at mowing lawns, but because I was a young man who looked him in the eye when I spoke to him. I got my first job because I listened to my dad's corrective voice.

I understand it's easier to listen to our parent's voice when we are kids, but the same principle applies here. When people you trust give you instruction for your life, don't get offended by it. Don't assume they're judging you. Do your best to embrace their words. Then go to God in prayer and ask him to reveal the truth about the matter. I wonder how much heartache all of us would have been spared if we had just listened to someone who was trying to warn us about the direction we were headed.

The bottom line is that judgment or correction is not such a bad thing after all. That is, if it is done with love and truth. God can use it to lead you closer to him. He can use it to improve your relationship with others. He can use it to bless you. Be open to correction and you will be better for it.

On the contrary, condemnation is a bad thing. It should not be furnished or tolerated by Christians. There is never a reason to give or receive condemnation. That's not our job. Condemnation is something Jesus would undo. Why don't we join him in that process?

CHAPTER NINE

Love Is the Answer "The Way It's Meant to Be"

"Darkness cannot drive out darkness: only light can do that. Hate cannot drive out hate: only love can do that."

—Martin Luther King Jr.

I have struggled with every one of the issues I've written about in this book.

Greed? Check.

Neglect? Check.

Hypocrisy? Check.

Impotent religion? Check.

Pride? Check.

Condemnation? Check.

I think the person I wrote this book for, at least to begin with, was myself. I needed to put pen to paper (or keys to computer) and write about the things God wanted to undo in my own life. There were walls in my world that should have come down long ago. I needed the hammer of truth to break through the barriers that separated me from God. Even worse, I needed that same truth to break down the walls I was unintentionally building that separated others from God. I certainly am not perfect. I still have a long way to go, but partly because of the time I have spent on this book, those walls aren't quite as high as they used to be. With the power and grace of Jesus, we will destroy the remaining walls together. It is his love and specifically his pursuit of my heart that makes all of this possible.

In my spiritual journey, few things have impacted me as much as the reality of God's unconditional love. By nature I'm a performer. I don't mean performing musically, although I do that sometimes. I really mean spiritually. I thought (and sometimes still think, unfortunately) that how well I do at what I do defines the amount of love God has for me. If I do well, God loves me a lot. If I don't do so well, his love lessens. That sounds crazy to me when I hear myself say it. Sometimes, however, it has been as easy for me to believe that God's love is conditional as it is to believe the sun rises each morning. I used to think I could earn God's love with performance.

Playing to the Crowd
That warped thinking didn't start with God, though. It started with sports.

Early on in my life I began to notice that if I did well at a sport, people liked me. Maybe they even loved me. People were simply being encouraging, but for an approval junkie like me, it was like a drug. If I hit a home run in T-ball, people clapped. If I ran a touchdown in peewee league football, people cheered enthusiastically. If I pinned someone in a wrestling match, they gave me a medal and chanted my name.

I picked up on this quickly. I began to crave the approval of others. Being successful at sports was the perfect way to get the "love" I was seeking. I did well at sports, and it seemed as though people loved me for it. This was a nice unspoken contract between me and everyone else, even though no one else knew about it.

But this plan began to break down when I was thirteen. The baseball team I played on made it to the Dizzy Dean Little League World Series. That was a big accomplishment for a little team from Oklahoma. We had already won ninety baseball games that year and had only lost six. That's a lot of baseball in one summer, but all of us loved it. World Series, here we come.

When we arrived at the ballpark in Kosciusko, Mississippi, everything looked the same as it did at home. All the baseball fields had four bases, a fence in the outfield, and a pitcher's mound. They had dugouts, bullpens, and chalk on the base paths. It all looked the same, but it wasn't. This was the World Series. The stakes were bigger than they ever had been. Right then winning these games meant more to me than anything. And we were fortunate enough to win a lot during that tournament.

It's still hard to believe, but we cruised easily through the first four games. Incredibly, we were going to the finals of the World Series undefeated. We had already achieved more than any of us ever thought we would, but to play in the finals was a dream come true.

The score was 5–3 in the sixth inning of the final game. We were losing. Nothing had gone right that day. We couldn't hit. We didn't field the ball well. We just weren't sharp. To be fair, the team we were playing was really good. They had some of the best players I had ever seen at that age. They were fast and strong. A few of them looked like they were in their mid-thirties, with full facial hair and muscles like a body builder.

Still I thought we could beat them. So did the rest of our team. That's when it happened. We had a late sixth inning rally. We started hitting the ball and scoring runs. We played like we hadn't played so far that day. It was like someone just hit the power button on our team. By the end of that inning, we were ahead 7–5. We only played seven innings at that age, so we just had to hold them off for one more inning.

That inning played out like a movie scene. In the last few moments of the game they were up to bat and had already scored one run. That made the score 7–6. We had two outs. Bases were loaded. Their best hitter was up. We hadn't been able to get him out all day. I was the catcher, so I called for a fastball on the outside corner, away from this guy's sweet spot.

Where do you think the pitcher threw the ball? Right down the middle of the plate.

The next few seconds seemed like they happened in slow motion. The hitter rocked back on his heels, tightened his grip, and took a swing at the ball. WHACK! He hit that ball so hard and high I didn't think there was any chance of it staying in the ballpark. Our center fielder instantly started running back toward the fence. The ball was sailing out toward the warning track. I just knew it was a home run. A hush came over the crowd. Then, standing near the fence, our center fielder opened his glove and . . . he caught the ball for the final out.

We were World Series champions!

Friends, my world at that moment turned into pandemonium. We sprinted toward each other as fast as we could. Then we started piling on each other. We were jumping on one another like WWF wrestlers coming off the top rope. This was celebration at its finest. The parents got in on it as well. Our little team from Oklahoma had done the impossible. We had won the World Series.

My dad made his way onto the field and locked eyes with me. He swung open that chain link fence and ran toward me. Then he threw his arms around me and all my catcher's gear, and he bear-hugged me.

What a moment! One I will never forget.

I had achieved something spectacular in my life. I thought this was going to be the epitome of feeling loved. I couldn't perform at a higher level at that age in baseball. I had made it to the top. At thirteen I had arrived.

But I was wrong.

The satisfaction of the win was nice, but the love from everyone around me was temporary. It didn't last long at all. It wasn't supposed to. I can see that now, but I couldn't see it then. Having the cheers die down was discouraging to me. I did the only thing I knew to do. I got back on the hamster wheel of achieving in sports and continued performing for the love and acceptance of others.

Now for the quick version of what followed. Through a miraculous set of circumstances, we went back to the World Series the next year. It's hard to believe, but we won the championship again. Same story. We were underdogs. We made it to the finals. We won. Celebration. Awards. Excitement. But again it was short-lived. The expiration date on this kind of love was much shorter than I wanted it to be.

Was there something better than this? If there was, I hadn't found it yet.

So as a teenager I continued to play sports. Performing for love and acceptance came as natural as gravity for me. I was an All-State football player my senior year and had received and accepted a scholarship to go play football and baseball in college. I loved playing sports, but I also loved the fact that it caused other people to like me. Long before I realized it, my identity was wrapped up in my reputation as an athlete.

Performance-Based Love

All the while God had been working in my heart. He was quietly calling me into a deeper relationship with him. I worked at a church the summer before my freshman year in college. I had also been working out and getting ready for football two-a-days starting in August. I was in the best shape of my life. Through the help of a friend, though, I was starting to feel like the right thing to do was go to a small Bible school in Oklahoma.

I really didn't want to. I was an athlete. I was good at sports. This small college wasn't known for its sports program. It was known for, well, studying the Bible. Can't I do that on my own time? And if I didn't play sports anymore, who would I be? More importantly, would anyone like me?

Although I didn't understand it, when I prayed about it, I felt like God was directing me to Hillsdale Bible College. I told my parents what I was thinking, and they couldn't believe it. They didn't understand it either. I had never talked about going to Bible college before, so the idea blindsided them. After a little time and some convincing, though, they said they would support whatever decision I made.

Because I was convinced that the decision really was made for me by the Lord, I had to accept it. So I gave up the sports scholarship and went to Hillsdale to major in theology. The school didn't have a football team, and our baseball team was 11–60. Even with a team full of preachers, prayer couldn't improve a team that bad. It was a new experience for me. I had no idea where my life or my career as an athlete was headed.

When I got to college, nobody really knew me. I had no reputation other than what a buddy of mine had told a few of his friends who were going to school there. It felt weird. They didn't know me as an athlete. They had not seen a high school highlight reel of my sporting endeavors. I was just Michael. And I didn't really like "just Michael." He wasn't all that interesting. The Michael that scored touchdowns, hit home runs, and had his name in the paper was interesting. The other Michael was just a guy. No one would love just a guy.

So that's when I started playing guitar. But this had a twist to it. I was playing guitar for Jesus now. Out of sheer necessity, the student-body director asked me to lead worship one day in chapel. I said yes, but only because it was just a one-time thing. I wasn't great that day, but I did well enough to get the job done. Little did I know that God was preparing me to become a worship leader. It wasn't some dramatic moment when the voice of God came through the clouds and he spoke to me audibly. It was a fellow student who was in a bind and needed me to help him out.

That seemingly insignificant moment was the beginning of my desire to be a worship leader. I traveled some for the college, singing and leading worship at retreats and camps. It wasn't long before the band named FFH asked me to play and sing with them. They wanted me to move to Nashville and sign a record deal with them. I was just nineteen years old. I accepted this awesome opportunity, but something was unraveling in my life.

When I stopped playing sports, my identity started to suffer because I could no longer perform for love and acceptance. When I picked up the guitar and realized I could write and sing songs, this became my new identity. Now I was Michael the musician instead of Michael the athlete. I honestly thought God saw me that way too. As long as I could lead well, write well, and sing well, I thought God loved me more. I know it sounds crazy but I thought it was true.

I also read my Bible every day because I thought it made him love me more. I testified about my faith every chance I got because I thought this made him love me more. I constantly lived with the misconception that God could love me more than he did. I thought I could make God love me more or less by what I did or how I performed. This heresy is known as performance-based love.

Performance-based love says I can do something to earn or keep God's love. It is doing something in order to obtain God's affection. This mixed-up motive for good works is common among people in our churches. I've seen pastors, worship leaders, deacons, and countless church members practice this kind of theology. But this expression of faith has one major flaw in it. It is completely unbiblical.

We cannot earn God's love. We cannot do anything to keep it either. In fact the Bible says in Romans 5:8, "God demonstrates his own love for us in this: While we were still sinners, Christ died for us." That means that before we had a chance to prove how "worthy" we are, God had made his decision about us. He loved us.

If I became the best singer in the world or the worst singer in the world, God would not love me any more or any less.

If I became the best songwriter in Christian history or the worst songwriter in Christian history, God would not love me any more or any less.

If I became the most respected man on the planet or if no one respected me, God would not love me any more or any less.

His love isn't based on who I am but on whose I am. I am his son and he loves me unconditionally. Learning this was a life-altering moment of understanding for me. If my identity was in Christ and his love for me never changed, I was constantly loved. I was constantly his. I didn't have to earn his approval.

God's love made me feel safe for the first time in my life. It was like I had released the white-knuckle grip I had on performance and had begun to rest in his love for me. Oh, how I wish everyone could have that kind of moment in their life. We all need to rest and remain in the security and vastness of God's love.

God's Complete, Constant Love

Brennan Manning chimed in on this subject, too. I heard him tell a story about being passed out, drunk, at the bottom of an outdoor stairwell. His head was leaning up against a trash-can, and his hand was clutching a bottle of vodka in a brown paper bag. A little boy walked by and noticed Brennan. The boy pointed at him and said, "Look, Mama." His mother furiously scolded her son and told him not to look at "that trash." Then she covered the boy's eyes and walked him away from where Brennan was lying. I remember Brennan saying that even in the midst of that horrible moment, with dried vomit on his face from the night before, God didn't love him any more or any less than he did now that Brennan was a noted author and speaker.

God's love never changes. It doesn't require us to get better, stand straighter, scrub cleaner, or sing prettier. He loved us from the minute we were conceived, and he loves us still. That love has never been altered, nor will it ever be. In my opinion our inability to understand this simple truth is one of the reasons many Christians only experience a fraction of the life God intends for them. Not feeling fully loved leaves us scared and afraid. We will never live completely free as believers if we can't understand what Brennan Manning teaches in *All Is Grace*—that "God loves us as we are and not as we should be."

But he also loves us too much to leave us the way we are.

This is one of the reasons we have so many legalistic Christians. They don't understand God's love. They think they have to perform to merit God's love, so they make you and me perform to receive theirs. To live in relationship with a person like this is exhausting and debilitating. I know, because I was one. This kind of Christianity is not what Christ lived and died to bring. It is but a shadow of the real life he intends for us to have.

God's love doesn't depend on our abilities. Whether we are the best athlete in world or the worst, God's love for us is the same.

God's love doesn't depend on our school grades. (Some of us can breathe a sigh of relief on that one.) Whether we are the best student in our class or the worst, God's love for us is the same.

God's love doesn't depend on our physical beauty. Whether we are a beauty queen or have never had a date in our life, God's love for us is the same.

God's love doesn't depend on our success. If we have made it to the top of the ladder or if we are struggling to get to the first step, God's love for us is the same.

God's love doesn't even depend on our spiritual devotion. Don't misunderstand me here. This isn't a license to do whatever we want because "God will love us." I certainly believe that a healthy relationship with God is built by spending time with him and obeying his teachings. But I am saying that if I read my Bible every day or if I never read it again, God's love for me will be the same.

His love doesn't change.

God's love doesn't always look like our parents' love. Keely and I don't have kids yet, but from what I understand, the way a parent loves their child is the best model we have on this earth of how God loves us. Most parents will do anything for their kids. They love them unconditionally. But if I read the Scriptures correctly, the way a parent loves their child is just a crack-of-the-door glimpse at how God loves us. God's love is deeper than what we can experience even in the most beautiful and heartfelt relationships on earth.

So what does this "perfect" kind of love look like? Here's how the familiar passage from 1 Corinthians 13:4–8 describes it:

Love is patient, love is kind. It does not envy, it
does not boast, it is not proud. It does not dishonor
others, it is not self-seeking, it is not easily angered,
it keeps no record of wrongs. Love does not delight
in evil but rejoices with the truth. It always protects,
always trusts, always hopes, always perseveres. Love
never fails.

Then there is the description Paul gives us in Romans 8:38–39: "For I am convinced that neither death nor life, neither angels nor demons, neither the present nor the future, nor any powers, neither height nor depth, nor anything else in all creation, will be able to separate us from the love of God that is in Christ Jesus our Lord."

We have never strayed too far to be outside of God's love. We have never done something so bad that God's love cannot reach us. No matter what we have done, no matter where we have been, God's love is constant. It never weakens. It never wavers. It is always the same.

Why do I spend so much time talking about God's love near the end of a *What Would Jesus Undo* book? Because if we haven't received God's love, both in our hearts and in our heads, how can we ever hope to pass his love on to others? How can we expect to love like Jesus, if we can't be loved by Jesus?

The Bible says in 1 John 4:19 that "we love because he first loved us." If we can understand and accept God's love, then we have a good chance of convincing others that God loves them too. They will see it in us. If they don't see it in us, why on earth would they want to be Christians? How could we ever undo the walls that exist between God and his people if we don't first live in his love for us?

I'm telling you: this is a life changer. I have never been more certain of anything. God's love coming to me and then passing through me is the most effective way to spread the gospel.

When you preach as someone who has been marked by God's love, it is his voice speaking.

When you care for the poor and broken as someone who has been changed by God's love, it becomes his hands caring for them.

When you give to others like someone who has been undone by the generosity of God's love, it is his heart showing through.

The love of God flowing to us and through us is the most convincing evangelistic tool we have.

A Father's Love

I'd like to close this chapter by telling you a story about my dad, Jerry Boggs.

When I think of God's love, I think of him. He's only six feet two inches tall, but he's a giant of a man to me. He'll probably never fully understand what he did for me several years ago on a summer day in Berryhill. But I can tell you this. I am able to love those around me better because of his love for me.

In the early 2000s, a friend of mine invited me to go listen to Brennan Manning one night, and I accepted. I was greatly moved by Brennan. He spoke about the love of Jesus so confidently that I bought one of his books and made a promise to myself that I would read it.

From the first page I was hooked. Sometimes I had to read the book with a dictionary beside me, because Brennan's vocabulary was far more extensive than mine, but I understood what he was saying loud and clear. Jesus not only likes you; he loves you. At some point in the reading, I came across a prayer Brennan often asked us to pray. It was very simple.

"Abba, I belong to you."

"Abba" means "Daddy" in Hebrew. In Bible days it was the term a child would use to address their father. The phrase has just the right amount of syllables, so that you can breathe in the word *abba* and breathe out the words "I belong to you." A prayer like this was intended to be repeated for as long as necessary. Sometimes such a prayer could be prayed for hours. I thought I would give it a shot. What did I have to lose?

I went to a quiet spot inside my house in Franklin, Tennessee, closed my eyes and said something like this.

"Father, how much do you love me?" That sounds like a prayer a father would want to answer.

Then I started praying in repetition:

"Abba, I belong to you."

"Abba, I belong to you."

"Abba, I belong to you."

Now brace yourselves, because this gets a little crazy for a Baptist boy. I believe that in that moment the Lord began reminding me of a time when I was a boy. I had just returned from vacation with my mom and my sister, Michelle. Branson, Missouri, had been the vacation destination for the Boggs family. We went there at least seventeen years in a row. Our family vacations usually were just the three of us. Dad worked hard to provide for our family and often couldn't take off work to go with us. But he always made sure we could go.

When we arrived back at our house, we had to tell Dad about all the fun we had. We always brought back a gift or trinket of some sort for him. We wanted him to know that we thought about him amidst all the excitement of our vacation.

On this particular occasion, Mom told Michelle and me to unpack our things and to settle back into the house. We did. Everything seemed normal.

I didn't pay much attention, but I did notice that Mom and Dad walked out of the house and toward the back of our two-and-a-half-acre property. They talked out there for a few hours. Obviously, they wanted to be alone. I thought they wanted to catch up on how the vacation went. I didn't ask any questions.

Eventually I heard my parents come in the back door. They called Michelle and me in for a family meeting. That was odd because we normally didn't have family meetings in our house. Nevertheless, we all filed into the living room and sat down on the floor.

I noticed Mom had been crying. Actually, she had been crying a lot. Her eyes were already swollen. Her cheeks were wet with tear-mixed-mascara that had run down her face. What had just happened? I wondered if maybe someone had died. That was the only logical explanation for that kind of tears.

My dad started talking first. He is a man who usually has no trouble finding the words to say what's on his mind. He's a straight shooter. But even my dad couldn't really get out what he wanted to say. After what seemed like an eternity, the bad news finally made its way out into the open.

"Your mom and I are going to get a divorce."

I looked over at Michelle, who had already started to cry. With tears streaming down her face, she folded her hands and started praying. I remember Dad being shaken up by the pain in her prayers. Even though Michelle was just a young teen, she was always more mature than her age gave her credit for.

I didn't know what to think. I was probably too young to understand what divorce meant. All I knew was that, shortly after that family meeting, Dad packed a bag and left. Mom said he was going to Grandma's house for a while.

I remember that all three of us slept in the same bed that night. Before we went to sleep, I asked Mom if Dad was coming back home tomorrow. Like I said, I guess I didn't really comprehend what divorce meant. She said she didn't think so. The next night was a carbon copy of the night before. We all slept in the same bed, and I asked the same question. "Is Dad coming home tomorrow?" Again, my mother said she didn't think so. Finally, although the third night was looking exactly like the previous two, when I asked if Dad was coming home the next day, Mom's response was different. She said he wanted to come by and talk to us the next morning.

I got up early that morning. I hadn't seen Dad in a few days, and I missed him. Looking through the window, I saw his truck pull up, but I also noticed that our pastor and his wife pulled in right behind him. After a few hugs and some pleasantries with the pastor, we sat down in the living room. I remember my dad's exact words. He's a country boy, so imagine him saying this with a country accent. "Preacher, I've been a sinner boy. And you can't have a good family when you've been a sinner boy."

That was Dad's way of confessing his sins. He then knelt down next to our pastor and gave his life to Christ. I'll never forget that day. It was one of the most amazing moments in my life. We were all overwhelmed with emotion and gratefulness to God. Mom and Dad's marriage took the first step toward healing. That has lasted forty-four years and is still going strong. Our little family was back together again.

Later that morning, we were all sitting Indian-style in the living-room floor, telling each other things we probably should have said a long time before that. I had never seen my dad cry, but when I looked over at him, he had tears running down his cheeks. He looked my sister and me in the eyes and said the words I'll never forget. "I love you guys," he said, "I'm sorry I've not told you that more, but I love you."

I'm now thirty-five years old, and that is my favorite memory. I can't begin to tell you what those words communicated to me that day and what they still communicate to me now.

Now, flash back with me. Remember earlier in the story? I'm still in my quiet time. I have been praying, "Abba, I belong to you," in repetition for at least an hour. God had been gracious enough to remind me of one of the most treasured moments in my life—the memory of my dad saying he loved me. Then I remembered a line from Brennan's book, *Ruthless Trust,* that I had read just prior to my prayer time. "Take your human feelings, multiply them exponentially into infinity, and you will have a hint of the love of God revealed by and in Jesus Christ" (19).

I didn't realize it then, but God was revealing his love for me through my dad. And the way my father loved me impacted how I love others. If we can allow ourselves to receive love, we're much more likely to be able to give it, aren't we? The love of God passes through us and into the lives of others.

Isn't it sad that some people sit in church every week but do not believe that God actually loves them? Our churches are full of people who sing praise and worship songs, give regular tithes, say amen during the sermon, but do not have the slightest clue how much God cares for them. This breaks my heart for two reasons.

How can we really love a God we don't believe loves us?

How can we show his love to others if we first haven't received it ourselves?

Jesus wants to break down all of the walls we've discussed in this book. But the wall that keeps us from receiving his love might be the most important one for us to undo. Whatever the barrier is in our lives, even a glimpse of the unrestrained love of God will make anything else pale in comparison. No amount of riches or possessions can compare with his love. It is free, but it isn't cheap.

Could it be that the one thing Jesus would undo in us is our inability to receive his love? Maybe he wants to undo our inability to show that love to others. I do know one thing. If we unleash into our world the beautiful fury of the love of God, life as we know it will change. It will change for us, and it will change for those around us. Grace will be far more prevalent than it is. Kindness won't be such a rarity. Hopelessness will have no hope of surviving in the climate of such love.

Allow God to love you. Allow that love to flow through you. It might be the only way the people around you will believe in him.

Whoever does not love does not know God, because God is love. This is how God showed his love among us: He sent his one and only Son into the world that we might live through him. This is love: not that we loved God, but that he loved us and sent his Son as an atoning sacrifice for our sins. Dear friends, since God so loved us, we also ought to love one another. No one has ever seen God; but if we love one another, God lives in us and his love is made complete in us (1 John 4:8–12).

CHAPTER TEN

A Letter from Me to You

Friends,

First of all let me say how grateful I am that you would take the time to read this book. I know you are busy. The fact that you took some of your personal time to skim or read through this book is an honor for me. I sincerely hope and pray that God will be glorified in and through your life. If this book has helped with that, my prayers concerning my writing have been answered.

I write to you now, not as an author or as a musician, but as a friend. I write as one who cares deeply about this beautiful thing called the church. My guess is that you do too, or you wouldn't have taken your free time to read a book about God and how we can better serve him.

For all the negative press Christians can get from time to time, I don't want us to forget that we do so many things well.

I am convinced that no one helps the poor like Christians do. I've personally witnessed hundreds of people who self-lessly give their time, money, and lives on behalf of serving the poor. Most have asked for nothing in return.

I believe we are among the fastest responders to human tragedy. When a hurricane or tornado hits somewhere in the United States, churches all over the country pull their resources together to help those in need. I was in Oklahoma in the summer of 2013 after several tornados devastated the city of Moore. There were many people helping clean up that city; but who was at the heart of it? Christians. Even several months later, who was still sending teams to assist people with rebuilding and restarting their lives? Christians.

When it comes to orphan care, I'm not sure anyone does it better than Christians do. Both domestically and internationally, many have given their lives to care for children who have nowhere to go and no one to go to. Are there still orphans? Yes. Are there a whole lot less of them because of Christians? Absolutely! I know many folks who have given up dream jobs and high paying careers for which they've worked hard, only to start a non-profit organization to help orphans. I also know many couples who have opened up their homes to adopt children who need a family. They selflessly give of themselves to care for those in need.

When it comes to helping the hurting, Christians do that well, too. Whether it's alcohol-abuse meetings or divorce-care classes, Christians are giving care and education to those who want it and need it. It takes people to teach those classes. It takes money to buy the materials. People donate a portion of their finances to make sure people who need help get it.

Christians care for the homeless well, too. Homelessness is a problem here in Nashville, where I live. According to Nashville Rescue Mission, there are over fifty-five thousand homeless men and women in Nashville every year. Fifty-five thousand! Volunteers organize ways to not only help these folks, but also to bless them. They offer work rehabilitation classes to get them back in the work force. They teach them new skills so that they can find jobs and take care of themselves. Best of all, they take care of them by giving them a place to sleep, food to eat, and spiritual direction until they are able to stand on their own two feet again.

Folks, the church is doing a lot of really good things. I would venture to say that many people who never attend church would even feel the same way about some of the things I have mentioned above. I want to encourage you in that. God is reaching people through the hard and selfless work of the church.

I tell you all of this to remind you that even in the midst of what Jesus would undo in our world concerning the acts and behaviors of Christians, God is very much at work in us. I don't want us to miss that truth. He's at work in us because he loves us and wants to reach the world through us. There are many things Jesus would undo in us; but it's not because he doesn't like us, it's because he loves us. He wants more for us than a cheap impersonation of Christianity. He wants us to have the real thing.

If we are going to continue undoing things in ourselves, our relationships, and our churches, I think there are a few things that will help us along the way. I want to suggest a kind of checklist of sorts to help make better decisions and align ourselves with the kind of decisions Jesus made. These are the Five Bs of WWJU:

1. Be brave. You are undoubtedly going to face walls that seem impossible to break down. Whether it's at your job, in your friendships, at your church, or in yourself, bravery is nearly always required to break through these barriers. Stand strong. Advance the kingdom of God by banishing fear and timidity with courage and trust in Jesus and his word.

Like Mary Anne Radmacher said, "Courage doesn't always roar. Sometimes courage is the little voice at the end of the day that says, 'I'll try again tomorrow.'"

Let your bravery lead you to conquer the strongholds in your life that have been places for the enemy to fly his flag. The beauty of bravery is that it is a characteristic of Jesus himself. Jesus faced fear head on many times. However, his trust in his father was unwavering. We are not brave because we are strong and mighty. We are brave because God is strong and mighty. "If God is for us, who can be against us?" (Rom. 8:31b). Be brave and tear down the walls that separate us from God.

2. Be forgiving. Forgiveness has the power to break down so many walls. I know some walls have stood for years because someone would not forgive the other. Outside of the obvious reason of God withholding forgiveness from you if you withhold it from someone else (Matt. 6:14–15), not practicing forgiveness is toxic to your own life. I remind myself often what Saint Augustine of Hippo wrote: "Unforgiveness is like drinking poison and hoping the other person dies." Max Lucado says it's like staying locked up in a prison cell to which you hold the key.

If you need to cry a million tears to forgive, then cry. If you need to have a conversation with the person to forgive, then make an appointment. If you need to pray through it, then get up every morning and take the time to ask God to help you extend forgiveness to someone.

Oftentimes the hardest person to forgive is ourself. Some of us can forgive the vilest offense done to us, yet harbor bitterness and won't forgive ourselves for petty little things. If God has forgiven you, forgive yourself. You'll be healthier and happier for it. Move on. Give the same grace to yourself that Jesus offers in these situations. Be forgiving. Too many walls exist because we simply don't forgive.

3. Be thankful. Nothing tears down the walls of comparison and discontentment like thankfulness. Thankfulness is like a wave that washes over all the frustrations we may have about our present situation.

I remember having a good friend tell me a story about when she received news that no young lady would want to hear. I won't go in detail, but this was devastating to her. When I asked her how she overcame her sadness, she began to tell me about a journal entry she made on a plane not long after she received the bad news. She told me she wanted to write down all the things she was thankful for. She began writing and filled up the first page. She continued and filled up the second page. She kept writing and writing and writing. Before her flight landed she had several journal pages of things she was thankful for and the presence of Jesus in her thankfulness had lifted her spirits.

I don't know your situation or what you're going through; but I do believe that when it comes to difficult times in your life, thankfulness is like a lifeline that will pull you out of the pit you're in. Practice being thankful. Let it be in your heart, on your mind, and on your lips. A heart full of thankfulness doesn't have room for self-pity and despair.

4. Be a good listener. Did you know that listening breaks down walls? I remember talking to a counselor friend of mine and he told me that the majority of his time is spent listening. He is a professional listener. People will often tell him how good he is at counseling. They'll recommend him to others because of it. He's had a reputable ministry and business in Nashville for years. Why? Because he's a good listener.

Sometimes people just need or want someone to listen to them. You don't always have to have the right words to say. You don't always have to have the perfect Bible verse or spiritual antidote. Oftentimes we need to listen and do our best to feel what other people are feeling.

Cry with them. That's what Jesus did for Mary when she told him about her brother Lazarus (John 11).

Pray with them. Sometimes the best way to help is to ask God for his advice and listen to what he says (Jer. 33:3).

Hurt with them. I can't tell you what it has personally meant for me to have friends who hurt with me. If I tell my friends of a situation that is particularly difficult for me to go through, I have often felt it is easier to make it through if I see the pain on their face, too. They are feeling what I'm feeling by listening to what I'm saying. Community in suffering is God's gift to help us bear the load we carry. Where does it start? By listening.

5. *Be loving.* I suppose we could write a million books on this subject and never get to the depth of its importance. But loving others is not only one of the two great commandments that Jesus gave; it's what he himself modeled for us in his journey on this earth. He didn't just say I love you, he proved it with his actions. I love the way 1 John 3:18 is translated in the Message: "My dear children, let's not just talk about love; let's practice real love."

Practicing real love is often difficult; but I have no doubt that when it is practiced, it breaks down enormous walls. It will undo things like hatred, jealousy, and racism. It can even penetrate the hardest heart. No matter who you are, where you've been, or what you've done, the commonality that unites us all is the desire to be loved.

Let people know you love them. Show them you love them. Even if it's uncomfortable for you, you should try. Give effort toward it. Love is not only expressed through words.

It's expressed by how you treat people. It's shown in your thoughts turning into actions. It doesn't always have to be "spiritualized," either.

Mow your neighbor's yard.

Invite someone over for a home-cooked meal.

Pay for the person's drink behind you at Starbucks.

Pat someone on the back.

Look a friend in the eye and encourage him or her.

Make somebody laugh.

As Bob Goff would do, "duck somebody." (Yes, you can send half a dozen baby ducks to people as a present. It will arrive on their doorstep three days later for about forty dollars. You can also "llama someone," but those are a little more pricey.)

Love shows up in all kinds of different forms and fashions; but the point is to show others that you genuinely care about them. Throughout the years, I have said that if my friends and family knew that I loved them, my time on this earth would have been well spent. Be a loving person toward others. It might be the best hammer we have to undo the walls of evil in this world.

So, be brave, be forgiving, be thankful, be a good listener, and finally, be loving. Those are the Five Bs of WWJU. If we as believers could put into regular practice these five things, can you imagine the change that would happen in our culture? Can you imagine the change that would happen in our churches? In our relationships? In us?

Oh, the revival that would sweep our homes and our houses of worship! Oh, the beauty that would flood our hearts and our lives through the Holy Spirit. Oh, the wonder of God that we might recapture! Oh, the innocence of worship we might return to! Oh, the ruins from strongholds that would lie at our feet, broken and destroyed forever.

Friends, let Jesus begin his work of undoing in us first. Let us pray for him to break through every wall that separates us from him. Let's join him in that process.

I've often enjoyed this quote from Edward Burke: "The only thing necessary for the triumph of evil is for good men to do nothing." Let's start doing something. Or should I say, undoing something.

I pray God's strength and blessing on your life as you begin this journey.

Sincerely,
Michael

P.S. If God is undoing something in your life you can be assured of two things. It's for your good and for his glory. Let the undoing begin!

CHAPTER ELEVEN

A Letter to the Skeptics

To all the jaded, confused, mistreated, skeptical, disillu-sioned, fed up, and downright-angry-with-Christians people out there, this chapter is for you.

I completely understand where you're coming from. I'm sure some things you have heard, seen, or experienced have been undeniably preposterous and have left a bad taste in your mouth for this whole Christian thing. To be honest with you, I have experienced some of those things myself. I have often felt discouraged by it. I'm bothered by the fact that we Christians can proclaim so confidently that Jesus is Lord and then live nothing like him. I'm bothered by the fact that I can do the same thing. I often joke that the apostle Paul was wrong when he said in the New Testament that he was the greatest of all sinners. I've met some of the greatest. Paul was nothing in comparison to them. But, frankly, I probably have Paul beaten too.

First, let me say that my purpose here is not to convince you that Christians don't do bad or wrong things. We do. Nor is my purpose to give you some sort of sales pitch to motivate you to see past the bad in Christians to get to the good in us. You shouldn't have to. Nor am I trying here to convince you that being saved gives us the right to act like the devil. That's completely wrong and unbiblical.

I simply want to say I'm sorry.

All of us know that things are happening in the lives of Christians that don't look at all like the life Jesus lived. Often I fail to live like Jesus did. I want you to know that up front. When I say that Christians fail, include me. I'm saying I fail.

I fail at loving my wife like I want to, because I'm selfish.

I fail at being there for my friends and family like I want to, because I work too much.

I often think far too much of myself and show it by the way I treat others.

I say things I shouldn't say.

I've gone places I shouldn't have gone.

I could go on and on, but you get the point. I don't measure up. I never have and never will. Honestly, it's not for lack of trying. It's not for lack of desire. I can say I sincerely want to do the right things, but often I don't. That's not an excuse, but it is the truth.

So if you're mad at Christians, I understand where you're coming from. I really do. But we might too quickly decide that because a few Christians have let us down in some way or another, then we can't trust any Christians. Some might even think we can't trust Jesus. This is what I'd like to address with you.

Not following Jesus because we've been let down by Christians or by the church is not a completely reasonable conclusion. Let me explain.

The validity of Christianity shouldn't be based on the actions of Jesus' followers. The validity of Christianity should be based on Christ himself.

Was Jesus perfect?

Was he sinless?

Was he without blame?

Did he suffer like a sinner for you and me to give us eternal life?

Did he desire to give us grace in exchange for our mistakes? Love in exchange for shortcomings? Hope instead of hurt?

If you answered yes to any of those questions, let that be your motivation to follow Christ. Christ offers forgiveness. His forgiveness extends to you and me in the same way it extends to the "bad examples" we talked about earlier. He offers real forgiveness. He offers the kind of forgiveness that forgets our faults. Could we not offer that same forgiveness?

Not trusting Christ because of the poor example of some Christians actually ends up hurting us more than them. In essence, we're letting others make the decision about who we follow instead of making that decision for ourselves. To say that Christianity is irrelevant because of the misbehavior of some Christians really doesn't make sense. Trying to get back at someone else by not following Christ only ends up hurting us.

Have you ever heard the expression, "That's like throwing the baby out with the bath water"? When we make these emotion-filled decisions, that may be what we're doing. We may be forsaking the whole of Christianity because of one particular incident. You don't make decisions like this in other areas of your life, do you? For instance, we use the Internet almost every day. Are there places on the Web that are bad? Yes. Is the Internet bad? No. Most of us listen to music every day. Is some music bad? Yes. Is all music bad? No.

What if we could trust in Jesus even when we're still a little skeptical of some Christians? What if we could look past the faults of others into the grace of Jesus that covers and cleanses all of our misdeeds? What if we could look at the life of Jesus?

Here are three short sentences I often repeat to myself. This might seem simple, but I think it's effective.

Forgive others.

Forgive yourself.

Trust Christ.

If we can do those three things, our lives would be impacted for the good and we would have more impact for the good on the lives of those around us.

I hope you have found my words to be sincere and worth a few moments of your time. I genuinely want what's best for you. I believe that what is best for all of us is Jesus.

I'll leave you with these beautiful words from a friend of mine who recently died of cancer. He said this often: Christ is all.

Michael

What Would Jesus Undo

Would God un-preach every sermon spoken in hatred
The kind with hell fire burning on their lips
Would He un-sing every sacred song of worship
When we sing but don't mean a word of it

Would He un-say every scripture said in anger
The kind that's used to hurt more than to help
Would He un-point all the pointed words and fingers
And hold up a mirror so we can point 'em at ourselves

Oh, the things we do in His name

I wonder if He shakes his head
And thinks that's not what I meant
What does hurting the hurting prove
If we're supposed to love
I wonder why we judge
When grace has graced us too
When it comes down to me and you
What would Jesus undo

Would He un-keep all the treasures that we're hoarding
Give a couple hungry mouths some food
Would He un-build all the walls the church keeps building
To keep all the sinners off our pews

Oh, the things we do in His name

I wonder if He shakes his head
And thinks that's not what I meant
What does hurting the hurting prove
If we're supposed to love
I wonder why we judge
When grace has graced us too
When it comes down to me and you
What would Jesus undo

[Bridge]

Love doesn't keep score
Love cares more for others than it does itself
When will we realize
Maybe open up our eyes and see
This ain't the way it's meant to be

I wonder if He shakes his head
And thinks that's not what I meant
What does hurting the hurting prove
If we're supposed to love
I wonder why we judge
When grace has graced us too
If it comes down to me and you
I pray we all would see the truth
And maybe ask a time or two
What would Jesus undo

Written by Michael Boggs and Jason Cox
©2013 Licketysplat Publishing / Simple Tense Music /
Winding Way Music / ASCAP

References

Bausch, William J. *A World of Stories for Preachers and Teachers: And All Who Love Stories That Move and Challenge.* Mystic, CT: Twenty-Third Publications, 1998.

Bono. "Keynote Address at the 54th National Prayer Breakfast." Delivered February 2, 2006. http://www.americanrhetoric.com/speeches/bononationalprayerbreakfast.htm.

Deem, Rich. "Hypocrites Defined: What about Hypocrisy in the Christian Church?" *Evidence for God.* Accessed March 24, 2014. http://www.godandscience.org/apologetics/why_are_christians_hypocrites.html.

DeYoung, Kevin. "Does Jesus Hate Religion? Kinda, Sorta, Not Really." *The Gospel Coalition.* January 13, 2012. Accessed March 24, 2014. http://thegospelcoalition.org/blogs/kevindeyoung/2012/01/13/does-jesus-hate-religion-kinda-sorta-not-really/.

Keith, Toby. Vocal performance of "Love Me If You Can." Written by Chris Wallin and Craig Wiseman. Recorded in 2007 on Big Dog Daddy. Show Dog Nashville B00JUJW8CU. Compact disc.

King Jr., Martin Luther. "Pride Versus Humility: The Parable of the Pharisee and the Publican." Sermon at Dexter Avenue Baptist Church, September 25, 1955. Accessed March 24, 2014. http://mlk-kpp01.stanford.edu/primarydocuments/Vol6/

25Sept1955PrideVersusHumilityTheParableofthe
PhariseeandthePublican.pdf.

Lewis, C. S. *Mere Christianity.* Colorado Springs: Harper Collins,
2011.

Manning, Brennan. *All Is Grace: A Ragamuffin Memoir.* Colorado
Springs, CO: David C. Cook, 2011.

——————. *Ruthless Trust: The Ragamuffin's Path to God.* New
York: Harper Collins, 2000.

Osborne, Larry. *Accidental Pharisees: Avoiding Pride, Exclusivity,
and the Other Dangers of Overzealous Faith.* Grand Rapids:
Zondervan, 2012.

Tchividjian, Tullian. "The Double-Reach of Self-Righteousness."
Liberate (blog). May 7, 2012. Accessed March 24, 2014. http://
www.tulliantchividjian.com/2012/05/07/the-double-reach-
of-self-righteousness/.

Van Dyke, Henry. *Valley of Vision.* Carlisle: The Banner of Truth
Trust, 1975.

"Vincent van Gogh." *The Biography Channel* Website. Accessed
March 24, 2014. http://www.biography.com/people/
vincent-van-gogh-9515695.

Willard, Dallas. *Divine Conspiracy: Rediscovering Our Hidden Life
in God.* New York: HarperCollins, 2009.

YOU HAVE THE POWER TO GIVE HOPE AND TO HELP MILLIONS OF CHILDREN AROUND THE WORLD.

HOPE
IT STARTS WITH
YOU!

Help today!
www.feedthechildren.org

FEED THE
CHiLDREN®